P9-CEM-604

Escape from Intimacy

OTHER BOOKS BY ANNE WILSON SCHAEF

Women's Reality

Co-Dependence: Misunderstood, Mistreated

When Society Becomes an Addict

The Addictive Organization (with Diane Fassel)

Meditations for Women Who Do Too Much

ESCAPE FROM INTIMACY

The Pseudo-Relationship Addictions

Untangling the "Love" Addictions:
Sex, Romance, Relationships

ANNE WILSON SCHAEF

HarperSanFrancisco
A Division of HarperCollinsPublishers

ESCAPE FROM INTIMACY. Copyright © 1989 by Anne Wilson Schaef. All rights reserved. Printed in the United States of America. No part of this book may be used or reproduced in any manner whatsoever without written permission except in the case of brief quotations embodied in critical articles and reviews. For information address HarperCollins Publishers, 10 East 53rd Street, New York, NY 10022.

FIRST HARPERCOLLINS PAPERBACK EDITION PUBLISHED IN 1990.

Library of Congress Cataloging-in-Publication Data

Schaef, Anne Wilson.
  Escape from intimacy.

  1. Relationship addiction.   2. Love—Psychological aspects.   3. Intimacy (Psychology)   I. Title.
RC552.R44S33   1989   158'.2   88-45698
ISBN 0-06-254860-3

ISBN 0-06-254873-5 (PBK)

03 04 05 RRD-H 20 19 18 17 16

To all those who wish to embrace intimacy
with themselves and others.

Contents

Acknowledgments   ix
Introduction   1

1. Sexual Addiction   9

2. Romance Addiction   46

3. Relationship Addiction   75

4. Escape from Intimacy   101

5. Addictive Relationships   114

6. Intimacy and Healthy Relationships   123

7. Recovery   143

Notes   159
Bibliography   161

Acknowledgments

I wish to thank the many persons who have so unsparingly shared their dreams with me. It is those who have so courageously sighed with relief at recognizing they are sex or romance or relationship addicts who have encouraged me to write this book, for they know that recognition of their disease process opens the doorway to recovery and intimacy.

I want to thank the participants in my intensives and workshops in the United States and in Europe and the American and German training groups for their support, insights, and feedback. They have encouraged me with their own lives and recovery. Without their help and input, this book could never have been written.

A special thanks goes to my agent, Jonathon Lazear, who said, "Do it," when this book was not on my agenda and to my editor, Jan Johnson, who, again, gave her unfailing support.

I hope what is written here adds another piece to our understanding and proves as useful to readers as it has been to those who have read the manuscript on two continents.

I thank all of you, especially my family, Beth, Rod, Di, John, Trish, and Tom, and my professional backups, Gwen and Mary Ann, for being there for me once again.

All of the cases and examples I refer to actually occurred and are accurate. However I have changed the names, locations, and identifying details. Most examples are composites of actual people and experiences.

Introduction

As a society, we are involved, I believe, in a very crucial process of learning about the range, focus, and impact of addictions on individuals, families, institutions, and entire cultures. We are beginning to understand that since we live in an addictive society, we have all been exposed to and trained into an addictive process. This addictive process is not a normal state for the human organism. It is something that we have learned.

It is of utmost importance to be aware that this underlying addictive process is culturally based and learned. It functions under rules of its own, rules that could be compared to flowing water finding its own course. We all know that when a stream is blocked, it will find its own way (frequently into our basements!). It is not that the water goes away when its path is changed; it just finds another, sometimes less convenient, way to express itself. The addictive process is much the same. If one path for its expression is cut off, it finds another.

We have also learned that addictions rarely, if ever, exist in isolation. After we have faced off against our favorite addiction, the one that is killing us or destroying our lives the fastest, and have attained a modicum of sobriety with that addiction, we discover our next most favorite, the one that is killing us the next fastest. We must move in our recovery from one addiction to another for two major reasons: first, we have not recognized and treated the underlying addictive process, and second, we have not accurately isolated and focused upon the specific addictions.

Usually we find that we have only worked with the specific addictions and have yet to address simultaneously the underlying addictive process *and* the specific addiction. When we only deal with the specific addiction, we tend to switch from one addiction to another or to have "cross-addictions" (a popular new term originally used to describe, for example, an alcoholic who is also addicted to cocaine). We must face each of the specific addictions and the underlying addictive process *together and separately* for recovery to proceed. Since traditional medical, psychological, and counseling techniques are singularly ineffective with most addictions and may, indeed, exacerbate the problem, we must face addiction as addiction and accept the reality of an underlying addictive process.

In my experience, the chemical and/or ingestive addictions have been the first to be confronted both historically and individually.

Then, in order for recovery to proceed, one must also confront the process addictions in which one is addicted to a process. These are addictions, for example, to work, money, sex, relationships, romance, religion, exercise—in which the focus is not upon the ingestion of a chemical or other substance. Process addictions are much more subtle and tricky than substance addictions, and they are very well integrated into our society. The more we learn about process addictions, the more aware we become that they are just as destructive and ultimately fatal to individuals, families, institutions, and societies as substance addictions. We must understand them and treat them with as much concern as we do ingestive addictions.

I completely agree with Patrick Carnes when he says in *Out of the Shadows*: "It may be that one of the greatest, unacknowledged contributions to recidivism in alcoholism is the failure of treatment programs to treat multiple addictions."[1]

In order to comprehend and work with the specific addictions, we must understand each specific addiction for what it is and see how each interacts with and supports the others. In addition, we must understand the relation of each addiction to the underlying addictive process.

We are just beginning to recognize some of the more subtle process addictions. Only as the more blatant substance addictions are confronted do process addictions begin to emerge. Some of the addictions that are beginning to get more attention lately are those that play themselves out in relationships or, to put it more accurately, pseudo-relationships.

We are beginning to see a whole range of books on relationship addiction, sexual addiction, loving too much, loving too little, looking for love, and similar topics. I am thrilled to see so much helpful material emerging on these subjects because addictions that play themselves out in pseudo-relationships are very common, affect many people in our society, and generate much pain.

At this stage of our knowledge and understanding of the addictive process, we need as much material from as many perspectives as we can get. No one has the final truth on this subject, and all of us bring pieces that add to our general understanding.

I have worked with many people who play out their addictions in pseudo-relationships, and I know personally and professionally how painful these addictions can be. The people who are struggling with these relationship forms of the addictive process deserve the help of as much information as it is possible for us to gather.

I have long been interested in addictions of pseudo-relationship and have been writing newsletters on these topics for the people who train with me. Though I did my first writing on the subject in 1984, and I had been speaking on addictive relationships for some time prior to that, I had never felt the need to write a book on the subject. However, as I read the recently published books (and some soon to be published) I came to the conclusion that, although most are excellent and add significantly to our knowledge, there are major pieces of information missing and perspectives not presented that I think are essential in understanding this cluster of addictions.

First, most of the books in the field combine and thus confuse what I think are three separate addictions, addictions that have a different genesis and a different focus, although they may interrelate significantly.

It is my experience that sex, romance, and relationship addictions are *separate* addictions, and all three can find their expression in addictive relationships. However, in order to understand "the nature of the beast," it is necessary to explore each separately and also look at the interrelationship among them.

As I stated earlier, these addictions are extremely tricky. They are not as blatant as chemical addictions, and unfortunately, they are subtly integrated into our society. They are also seductive. One can become almost voyeuristic and/or judgmental in discussing sexual addiction and lose contact with the reality that sexual addicts are persons who have a progressive, fatal disease and are in a great deal of pain; that they are just like other addicts. When addictive relationships are the norm for relationships in an addictive society, it is difficult to establish the reality that persons who are enmeshed in addictive relationships are both destroying those around them and are themselves being destroyed, in much the same way as alcoholics. When romance is continually sexualized, it is not so easy to see that sexual addiction and romance addiction are separate *and* related. Yet how easy it is for romance addicts to read the current literature on sex and "love" addiction and "not identify" with being sex addicts, thus missing the possibility of help for a disease that is destroying their lives. To complicate matters, most people would much rather admit to romance or relationship addiction than to sexual addiction. Many recovering alcoholics I know, for example, are much more willing to be alcoholics than sex addicts. There is more shame attached to sexual addiction.

Second, addictive relationships are not the same as sex, romance, and relationship addictions; sex, romance, and relationship addicts *form* addictive relationships as do other kinds of addicts. For recovery to progress, we need to look both at addictive relationships and their dynamics and also at the specific addictions that lead into addictive relationships.

As we separate out these three addictions and relate them to addictive relationships, I believe that we can gain more understanding and thus a greater possibility of recovery. As we read the stories of people like us, we can begin to see how these subtle, culturally supported addictions are destroying our lives.

It is tempting to focus on the "acting out" aspects of these addictions, especially the sexual addictions. They are the more sensational, the more "interesting" for the public (especially a sexually addicted public).[1] Yet I believe it is important to remember that the person who is "hooked" on sexual fantasies or who is a "sexual anorexic" is frequently in just as much pain and is just as destructive of relationships and of other persons as the child molester. Equally, the romance "junkie" is hurting and cannot completely deal with that pain through the rage of being a victim. These are forms of addiction, of the addictive process, and need to be treated as such.

Unfortunately, many of the discussions of these problems are lengthy, very clinical in nature, and not easily understood. These are helpful; there is much to learn and much to understand. Yet I believe it is important to see that many issues that we formerly perceived as psychological problems are, indeed, expressions of an addiction and can only be addressed as such. Moreover, the information should be readily available to everyone. We need to reiterate that addictions are not matters of morality; they are progressive, fatal diseases.

Along with the clinical discussions there are excellent books emanating from self-identified addicts, such as a book from the Augustine Fellowship that I find important.[2] Both perspectives on these issues are important. We also need books that have the clinical perspective and are read directly with the "gut." To recover, we need to identify with the disease. Since my book on codependence came out so many people have told me, "I found myself on every page."[3] That may not be true for this book, and I hope those who do need to find themselves here will.

I am concerned that current books do not adequately help us see the way these addictions relate to and are encouraged by our culture. There are some excellent explorations of the family dynamics that contribute to sexual addictions and addictive relationships, and I believe that these explorations do not go far enough. For recovery to truly progress, we need to see how sexual, romance, and relationship addictions are generated by our families *and* our schools, our churches, our political system, and our society as a whole. To stop with the influence of the family is to stop too soon. Where do families learn how to be families? Partially they learn from their families of origin, and they also learn from the institutions of the society. This needs to be acknowledged and explored in order for us to work effectively with these addictions.

In trying to isolate and understand sex, romance, and relationship addiction, I have realized that we need to take another look at the concept of co-dependence and co-sex addicts. Most people would rather be a "co-" than an addict. Yet is this labeling setting up or reinforcing a denial system that gets the person off the hook of facing relationship addiction as an addiction, for example? Isn't the co-sex addict also an addict, be it sexual, romance, or relationship? And is the reason we have had so much difficulty dealing with vagueness in the concept of co-dependency that we have confused several addictions and the underlying addictive process? All these questions need to be explored in relation to sex, love and romance, and relationship addiction.

In addition, when we are looking at the addictions that have their focus in pseudo-relationships, we need to see that though they look like ways of approaching intimacy, they are actually *escapes from intimacy*, ways of avoiding it. In order to understand how these addictions offer an escape from intimacy, we need to look at intimacy and healthy relationships.

Like Carnes, I believe that the addiction model may add greatly to our knowledge and may help us work with problems that have heretofore gone unnamed or for which traditional mental-health techniques have not been effective.[4] When we understand these addictions as addictions, we approach them differently.

I am concerned that we seem to use a simple cause-and-effect mentality to think about psychological problems. This approach makes it easy to fall into the illusion that if we just understand *why* people are the way they are then we (or they) can fix it. Hence, a great deal of effort goes into analysis of the problem and generation of data about family history and family patterns. Unfortunately, no one was ever cured of an addiction just by understanding it. In fact, the very process of "understanding" may be a way to "protect one's supply." I know that many people have been helped and relieved by that "Aha" experience of "So *that's* what's wrong with me," "That's my story," or "I see myself on every page." Yet that experience is only the beginning. Literally, it is only the first part of the first step of the Twelve Steps. When we face addiction as addiction, we then have the opportunity to begin our recovery, and recovery is a process, not an event.

I write this book to add to the information that is being generated about our escape from intimacy in the pseudo-relationship addictions. Chapters 1–3 discuss sexual addiction, romance addiction, and relationship addiction as separate addictions and show how each is related to our institutions and our society. Chapter 4 looks at the ways these three addictions interact and support one another. I will look at the concepts of co-dependent and co-sex addict as they relate to these three addictions and explore how each functions as an attempt to escape intimacy.

In chapter 5, we look at how addictive relationships are formed. Addictive relationships have some important dynamics, and I will discuss these in detail while simultaneously pointing out that addictive relationships are the norm for our culture.

Chapter 6 looks at some of the things we know about healthy relationships and some of the dynamics of healthy relationships. A discussion of intimacy in its various facets, essential to understanding healthy relationships, is also included.

Finally, in chapter 7 we look at the process of recovery from each of these addictions and what information we have about recovery from addictive relationships.

I want to thank all the people who have so generously shared their lives and stories with me and have encouraged me to write about their struggle. There have been many, and I feel honored and privileged to have been a part of their lives and their recovery.

The stories in this book are disguised and are composites to protect the identity of those sharing them, and the situations are real, as are the people involved. Their pain is real, as are their struggles.

1. Sexual Addiction

As I said earlier, there is an emerging awareness of sexual addiction and the destructive effects it has on the addict and on the object of a sexual addiction. The giant step we have taken in seeing and labeling sexual obsession as addiction is important for several reasons. First, addiction is a more accurate definition of sexual behaviors than are the purely psychological definitions. Second, the addiction model offers us the possibility of understanding a range of sexual behaviors that have been subtly integrated into the society as normal yet not clearly discussed and understood. Third, this approach offers us the opportunity of understanding the societal components of sexual addiction and the "commonness" of sexual addiction. Fourth, it offers hope and the possibility of recovery. Finally, this perspective allows us the possibility of understanding that sexual addicts are human beings who are hurting, who have a progressive, fatal disease that can wreak havoc on others and often does.

Characteristics of Sexual Addiction

As we often see when we are trying to understand an old phenomenon from a new perspective, there are a range of definitions of sexual addictions. I believe that this diversity of definitions is important and adds to our knowledge and understanding. At this point in the development of our knowledge, there is no need to have one, clear succinct definition on which we can all agree.

Patrick Carnes says, "The addict substitutes a sick relationship to an event or process for a healthy relationship with others. The addict's relationship with a mood-altering 'experience' becomes central to his life."[1]

Charlotte Eliza Kasl says, "Addiction is, essentially, a spiritual breakdown, a journey away from the truth into emotional blindness and death." Further, "I believe the epidemic proportions of sexual addiction and co-addiction in this culture reflect the spiritual breakdown of patriarchy which is based on the exploitation of all women." She goes on to say, "Sexual addiction is about more than relationships or pairing. It is a state of mind and a set of beliefs that can exist separately from other people. It is a relationship with oneself."[2]

Both these writers' definitions emphasize important aspects of a sexual addiction. Sexual addiction, like any other addiction, is mood altering. It affects the individual like any mood-altering drug. Sexual obsession becomes a "fix," and addicts get their "high" from the sexual fix.

Addicts become progressively more preoccupied with the sexual "fix" until it becomes central to their lives. As the disease progresses, the sexual obsession takes more control of the person's life, and more and more time and energy need to be spent in the sexual activity in order for the addict to get the same high.

In sexual addiction, as in all other addictions, there is a loss of spirituality and a breakdown of the addict's own personal morality. There is a progressive movement away from truth. As with any other addiction, the addict moves away from reality and toward the state of "insanity." Any addict becomes progressively "insane." As the thinking and the behavior of an addict moves further and further away from reality, thinking processes become impaired. This impaired thinking process is based upon faulty beliefs, confusion, distortion, justification, and illusion, and it moves sexual addicts still further from reality and from their own value system.

Sexual addiction is a progressive disease and as I will show later, results in destruction and early death for addicts and often those with whom they are involved. Sexual addiction is of epidemic proportions in this society and is integrated into the addictiveness of the society as a whole. No treatment of sexual addiction can be complete unless it explores the role of the society and the institutions of the society.

Sexual addiction exists within the individual and is different from romance addiction and relationship addiction. These addictions may interest and overlap and still they are not the same. I believe that it is imperative to understand these addictions separately as well as in relation to one another.

I believe that sexual addiction is an obsession and preoccupation with sex, in which everything is defined sexually or by its sexuality and all perceptions and relationships are sexualized. It is progressive and fatal. In all its forms, sexual addiction is destructive to the self, to others, and to relationships. Sexual addiction is a source of pain, confusion, and fear for the addict and also for those with whom the addict attempts to relate. Like all other addicts, sexual addicts become progressively dishonest, self-centered, isolated, fearful, confused, devoid of feelings, dualistic, controlling, perfectionistic, blinded to their disease (denial), insane, blaming (projection), and dysfunctional. In short, their lives become progressively unmanageable.

Sexual addiction, like all other addictions, is one expression of an underlying addictive process that has many forms of expression. As I stated earlier, we all have been exposed to and trained in the addictive process. Note that we have been trained in the addictive process; it is not core to our being. It is not who we are; it is what we have learned to be to fit into an addictive society. If we confront sexual addiction for what it is—an addiction—recovery is possible.

Sexual addiction is a hidden addiction; I have found more willingness to confront almost any other addiction. Sexual addiction carries a particularly large component of shame and denial with it. Paradoxically, it is also one of the addictions that is most integrated into our society as "normal."

It is only as the courageous persons with this addiction have come forth and named their addiction that we have been able to see the pervasiveness of this disease and the extent of the pain and suffering associated with it. Labeling this addiction a psychological illness allowed it to stay hidden. That process "protected the supply." Only as sexual addicts themselves have identified their addiction have we come to understand this progressive, fatal disease for what it is.

Much attention has been given recently to the acting-out aspects of sexual addiction (which, in itself, may be a form of sexual addiction called voyeurism). I plan to explore the full range of sexual addictions and the relation of sexual addiction to the institutions of our society and to our society as a whole. We cannot understand sexual addiction unless we look at the role of the family, the school, and the church as well as the society as a whole in this pervasive, fatal addiction.

Range of Sexual Addiction

As I stated earlier, most writing has been about sexual acting out in one form or another. Carnes does an excellent job of describing three levels of addiction from the less legally and publicly sanctioned to the more destructive to other people. Severe addiction and death can occur on any level.

According to Carnes, "Level One behaviors have in common general cultural acceptance. . . . Each can be devastating when done compulsively." He cites such behaviors as masturbating, looking at pornography, going to strip shows, and patronizing prostitutes. He also describes Level One relationships as those in which "one partner sacrifices important parts of the total relationship in the service of sexual needs," and homosexuality (I do not support his view on same-sex relationships).

"Level Two addictive behaviors are sufficiently intrusive to warrant stiff legal sanctions."[4] Under this level he lists voyeurism, exhibitionism, voyeur-exhibitionism, making indecent telephone calls, and "taking liberties."

Carnes's Level Three includes behavior even more illegal, intrusive, and destructive to others. As he says, "The common element of Level Three behavior is that some of our most significant boundaries are violated. Rape, incest and child molesting are basic transgressions of laws designed to protect the vulnerable."[5] Along with these three, Carnes includes other sexual violence such as sadomachism, sexual torture, and acting out toward the innocent.

Carnes does an excellent exploration of these levels. Since I have found his treatment to be helpful and thorough, I see no need to repeat here what he has written and can only suggest that if you want to look at his approach you read *Out of the Shadows*.

However, from my experience of working with a range of sexual addicts, I want to explore some forms of sexual addiction that are rarely mentioned or explored in the material now available.

Stories of Sexual Addicts

Sexual Anorexia

Molly is a tall, striking professional woman in her early forties. She is always tastefully dressed and, in general, appears to be competent, organized, and successful. Although she talks about feeling insecure and unsure of herself and her lifework, most people respond to her as a leader and a person they can admire, someone who is well on her way to "having it all together" if indeed, she doesn't already.

Molly has been married for twenty years and appears to have a stable family with three children. She and her husband, Jim, for all intents and purposes appear to have a "normal" relationship (and perhaps it is, statistically!).

As Molly talked about herself and her life, I began to see a very different picture from the one she presented to the world. Molly described her relationship with her husband as dead. She felt that they had a "form" marriage: they did all the right things and went through the motions of having a relationship, but there really was no intimacy and no relationship. She and her husband never talked, and most of all they never showed or expressed feelings. Molly had often thought about leaving her marriage, but according to her, she stayed because so little existed in the marriage that she could never really get a clear picture of what she would be leaving or staying in, so she stayed "stuck."

Molly is a recovering co-dependent. When she first learned about the concept of co-dependence, she was overjoyed to have a label for what she had been feeling most of her life. She was a person who always had looked for her definition outside herself. She had expected her family of origin, her work, her husband, and more recently her children to give her the definition that she did not feel inside herself. She also was a caretaker. In fact, a large part of her definition of herself was as one taking care of others. She believed that to take care of herself would mean that she was selfish and un-Christian. One of the ways that she took care of her husband was to "service" him sexually—to have sex when he wanted to even though she found it very difficult to be sexual.

Molly rarely, if ever, enjoyed sex, yet she felt that this was her own inadequacy and must be hidden from her husband because she did not want *him* to feel inadequate. She even faked orgasms to add to his pleasure. Of course, as a co-dependent, Molly was dishonest about her feelings and tended to control herself and others, especially in sexual areas.

Molly and Jim, understandably, never talked about their sexual relationship or nonrelationship, so both suffered under the illusion that it was normal, if unsatisfactory.

As Molly worked on her recovery from co-dependence, things began to change. She began to see that her extreme need for the approval of others left her without any awareness of or connection with a self that she could call her own. It also meant that others were left confused about who she was. In her recovery Molly began the slow process of finding out who she was, what she liked and did not like, and what was important to her. She shifted the focus of her control from being fairly evenly divided between herself and others to others and began to assert herself. She learned that she could say no when she wanted to and, in fact, may even have gone a bit overboard in her nay-saying for a while just for practice.

As Molly claimed her disease of co-dependence, she began to reclaim herself. She was a feminist and had put much energy into feminist pursuits and interests. As she recovered, she could see that much of her focusing "out there" to try to change others was an expression of her disease of co-dependence and control and allowed her to avoid the long struggle to define herself and to own her own power and identity. Paradoxically, as she claimed her own disease of co-dependence and the ways that she complied with and unknowingly supported the addictive system, she developed more self-esteem and felt more powerful and less like a victim. She began to see how she could change the system by first recovering from her disease. Molly was feeling good about herself, and her life was feeling more manageable.

Molly's family life was beginning to change also. She found herself less willing to have sex with her husband when she did not want to, and she felt more comfortable with herself and who she was. Of course, her changes had affected the family dynamics considerably, and there was more uproar in this formerly "normal," quiet family. Since Molly was the one who had been making the choice to change, Jim often blamed her for the "disease" in the family. Fortunately, her sobriety with her co-dependence was solid enough and she had enough support from many recovering friends that she did not accept the blame for her family's upset.

Suddenly, Molly's world was thrown into turmoil. One of her daughters reported that she and her brother had been involved in an incestuous relationship. The family acted immediately and sought the help they needed to deal with this family trauma. Molly strongly believes that her recovery from her co-dependence set the groundwork for this issue to come out in the open and be dealt with by the family. They now had broken through their denial system on several levels.

As each member looked at the family dynamics and the sexual issues in the family, both personally and collectively, Molly discovered that there was something lurking under her "co-dependence." She has described what she found deep inside her as her "sexual anorexia," and she has defined it as a sexual addiction.

Molly is obsessed with sex. She thinks about sex constantly. She finds it filthy, disgusting, dirty, and repulsive. Much of her time is focused upon how to avoid sex with her husband. In fact, she suspects that she may have developed an addiction to work (workaholism) in order to avoid sex ("too tired," "have to work," etc.).

Molly would like to *appear* sexual and attractive to men, but she does not want to *be* sexual. She might even be considered a rather prudish "tease." Whenever men approach her in any way, she sexualizes the interaction and is sure they only want one thing. Molly is afraid of men, afraid of sex, and terrified of her own sexuality. Formerly, we may have called her frigid. Unfortunately, like many of our psychological conceptualizations, the concept of frigid did not take in the element of addiction.

Molly now believes that her sexual addiction is at her very core. She also believes that her co-dependence covered up her sexual addiction and that she might never have faced it without first facing her co-dependence. Molly is very ashamed of her sexual addiction and finds her co-dependence infinitely more acceptable.

She says that it would have been easy for her to continue to be a "victim" of her husband's advances and to make him the culprit. Now she knows that she has a form of a progressive disease from which she can begin recovery. She very clearly states, "By owning my sexual anorexia, I am not saying that Jim does not have some form of sexual addiction also; after all, we did get together, didn't we? What I am saying is that I know that I have uncovered a form of sexual addiction in myself that is destroying my life. Jim is not my problem [well said for a recovering co-dependent]. He will have to look at himself and see what form of the addictive process he has and do his work. I can't do that for him."

When Molly talks of the pain and suffering that are related to her "sexual anorexia," it is easy to see that she is talking about a serious, progressive addiction.

Molly was in such extreme denial about sexuality and so confused and obsessed about her own sexuality that she was incapable of seeing what was happening in her own family. "Although I do not blame myself as the cause, I can see how my sexual anorexia blinded me to reality." Molly was so afraid of anything sexual that she refused to see sexual "clues" in her family. Moreover, since she tended to sexualize everything, she did not trust her perceptions when she did pick up something sexual in the family, and thus ignored it. Denial is a characteristic of addiction. Sexual denial is a characteristic of sexual addiction.

Like most anorexics, Molly became more and more isolated as she felt she had to hide her disease, and also like most anorexics she became progressively obsessed with matters that related to her anorexia—both characteristics of addiction. Although she wanted to be attractive, Molly took great pains not to dress seductively. In fact, she was so obsessed with seductiveness that the possibility of seduction completely ruled her life.

Molly never wanted to be sexual with her husband. She did not *want* to be celibate, she just did *not* want to be sexual. She was not going toward something, she was just going *away* from sexual. Hence her dishonesty and her need to control flourished.

Molly could even see her old friend perfectionism rearing its ugly head. If only she could find the *right* partner, under the *right* circumstances, with the *right* feelings, then, perhaps, she would feel all right about sex. But then she would always, eventually, feel the old revulsion.

Molly could see that her mother had conveyed to her that sex was disgusting and dirty and that her church had perpetuated this notion; she could also see that her society sexualized everything. Yet she knew from the recovery work that she had done on her co-dependence that she was facing a full-fledged addictive process in herself, and that she had to treat it as such.

Molly is one of the lucky ones. Through her recovery work with her co-dependence she was able to name her addiction and begin a twelve-step program around her "sexual anorexia." She asked me specifically to tell her story because she knows that she is not alone in this form of sexual addiction and so much of the current literature focuses upon sexual acting out. Her feminist self asked me if I thought that generally the focus was more on the acting-out sexual addict because it seems there are more men in those categories. Perhaps, I do not know. I do know that there are both men and women sexual anorexics who are hurting, who are obsessed with sex, and who can be helped if they will recognize that they have a sexual addiction from which recovery is possible.

This form of sexual addiction may not be as dramatic as sexual acting out, but there is no question that Molly's pain and suffering are real. On the surface, it appears that it is only Molly's life that is deeply affected by this disease. Yet her addiction has also affected her relationship with her husband, her children, and others in her life. She has been so obsessed with and phobic about her own internal struggle that she did not see what was happening in her family. She has been so obsessed with sex that she has not been able to relate intimately with men or women. She has found fellowship and recovery in the twelve-step Sex and Love Addicts Anonymous Program. For Molly there is hope.

Addicted to Sexual Fantasies

Julian is a man in his mid-thirties who exudes a shy, handsome ruggedness and has a sad, wistful look in his eyes. When I first met him, he appeared to be carrying the weight of the world on his shoulders. When he first came to one of my workshops, he sat somewhat back from the circle and seemed to be shy and withdrawn, although he was a person people were naturally drawn to. As we went around the circle introducing ourselves, I noticed that he was holding his body very tight, quietly wringing his hands, and doing other things that looked like nervous fidgeting. When his turn to introduce himself came, he blurted out his name, said that he was from Montana, and then told us that he was a sexual addict and wanted everyone to know that about him early on. He then said, "Whew, I got that out, now I can relax. I have never said that I was a sexual addict except in my Sex and Love Addiction group. I came here to work on my sexual addiction and wanted to own my addiction early on."

This intensive took place several years ago before there was much information about or recognition of sexual addiction, and I could feel the stunned silence of the rest of the men in the group. My guess (later confirmed) was that immediate fantasies were triggered: "What in the world does he do?" "Does he molest little girls (or boys)?" "Are we safe with him?" "He must really be a 'sicko.'" "Is his addiction contagious?" That is, "Will his talking about his addiction push us to explore the possibility of our being sexual addicts also?" I could tell there was a lot going on under the masks of quiet openness I was seeing on the faces around the room.

"Julian," I said, "are you willing to share more about your sexual addiction and how it affects you?" "I will," he said, "although it is very difficult to talk about it. I believe this group is safe, and I know I need to talk about this addiction and work on it in order to recover. I feel so desperate that I am willing to do almost anything. A member of my Sex and Love Addiction group suggested that one of your intensives might help, so here I am."

Then his story began to unfold. Julian was a happily married man with a small child whom he loved dearly. He told us that he and his wife had a good relationship and he had never been sexually or emotionally unfaithful. Yet he was reaching a point where he believed that his sexual addiction could destroy both him and his marriage.

Julian was addicted to sexual fantasies. He had engaged in sexual fantasies as a young boy and found them intriguing and stimulating. When he was in his teens, he was shy, and many of his sexual "exploits" took the form of fantasy. He did not date much, and when he did, he was "good" and did not "impose himself" upon his date. In college, he dated more frequently and generally found his relationships with women to be warm, friendly, and affectionate. He did not consider himself a "stud," nor did he act like one. In general, from what he reported, he did not sexualize relationships. During this time, he indulged in his sexual fantasy life and felt that he "kept it under control."

He firmly believed that when he married (which he fully expected to do) and had his own family, he would no longer need his sexual fantasies. In time he did marry, and he believed his marriage was a good one. Unfortunately, marriage did not prove to be the antidote for his sexual fantasies. They continued.

He had now reached a point where he believed that he was "powerless over his sexual fantasies, and his life had become unmanageable because of them." He asked that the group take him seriously and not dismiss the pain of his sexual addiction.

He said that he could now see the progressiveness of the disease. His early sexual fantasies had been fairly benign and, as he put it, "harmless." However, over the years, they had become progressively violent, to a point where they were frightening to him and he was terrified that he would act them out and be violent to others or himself be hurt or killed. He had vowed many times to stop these fantasies and had been unable to do so. He had spent thousands of dollars on therapy and confided that not only had it not helped but he had become uncomfortable with what seemed to him to be his therapists' preoccupation with the *details* of his fantasies. He now believed that the progressiveness of the disease could prove fatal to him in many ways. Not only did he fear acting out his fantasies, but he recently had become so involved in his fantasies that he had had a serious automobile accident in which he could have been killed or could have killed someone else. He had a look of desperation in his eyes as he almost pleaded with the group to see how *serious* this was for him. There was not one person in the room who could not feel what he was saying even though his story did not fit our image of what a sexual addiction must be like.

The accident was not the only way Julian's addiction was affecting his life. He could not "control" when he indulged in sexual fantasies anymore, and his work productivity was being adversely affected. He even found himself missing work and sneaking off alone so he could indulge in fantasies. He did the same with his family time. He would feign illness or a headache so he could be alone and fantasize. Tears rolled down his cheeks as he told how he avoided spending time with his child because he felt so bad and unclean—and also so he could indulge in fantasy.

As we listened to this man, it was easy to see that he was powerless over his sexual fantasizing and that his life was, indeed, unmanageable. He was hurting and he was hurting badly. He tried to maintain what he thought was a normal sexual relationship with his wife, and he felt so bad about himself and so "crazy" that this charade was all but impossible. We saw his pain and we believed him. Julian was suffering from a progressive, fatal disease that was in its chronic phase. Julian was a sex addict, even though he had never engaged in any activity that would usually be seen as sexual addiction. His sexual addiction was destroying his life, and he knew it.

When we met, he was working a strong twelve-step program and had a good sponsor. He knew that he needed all the help he could get, which for him included others' recognizing and accepting his addiction. He had found this in SLAA (Sex and Love Addicts Anonymous). Now he felt free to share his story with other twelve-step fellowship groups as he worked on subtler aspects of his addictive process. Julian is in recovery. Breaking through his denial and naming his disease have been the first step. He is not a bad person. He has a progressive, fatal disease.

Again, it is easy to see that what Julian described is a sexual addiction. But it is not what we usually think of as a sexual addiction, and he was in the chronic stage of the disease.

Julian had become progressively dishonest with his family, friends, his employer, and himself. He had become more and more isolated, and his ability to support himself and his family was threatened. He had lost weight because he had become so depressed about his inability to "control" his fantasies that he "forgot" to eat. He feared losing his job, his relationship with his wife, and his relationship with his child. Those fears were not unrealistic. His thinking patterns had become obsessive and paranoid, and he had begun to feel and act insane. Yet he had not really "done" anything, so for a long time he did not even consider the possibility that he is a sex addict. He has found tremendous relief in naming his disease. His story left no confusion about the progressive, fatal nature of this addiction. He was living proof that this form of sexual addiction can be as destructive as other forms and that he was a man who had "hit bottom" and was on his way out the other side.

I think it is important to see from Julian's story that sexual addiction is not necessarily relationship addiction. Sexual addiction may get played out in addictive relationships, and sexual addiction exists in its own right. One does not necessarily require another person or an object. Sexual addicts can be sexual addicts all by themselves. Many act it out on others, often innocent people, and we need to see that the other is not necessary for the addiction to exist. Sexual addicts do not always act out. Sexual addiction always results in neglect of the self, even when it seems totally self-centered. Like other addictions, it shuts off feelings, awareness of the self, and the needs of the self. In fact, the purpose of addiction is to put one out of touch with oneself. The sexual addict becomes progressively numb, and like other addicts, requires more to get the "fix." So it is with sexual fantasies as well as other sexual addictions.

Celibacy as Sexual Addiction

Aloysius is a Catholic priest. He has been in the priesthood for many years and is considered to have made major contributions in his work with native people in Central America. He is committed to the priesthood and the church. For him, this means that he has made a vow of celibacy and must remain celibate. Unfortunately, this is not an easy task for him. He suffers greatly with his celibacy, and he suffers greatly with his sexuality. In fact, Father Aloysius is obsessed with his sexuality and his celibacy.

Father Aloysius has had sexual affairs with two women in his parish. He feels tremendous guilt over these affairs and has broken off both even though he feels that he loved both women.

Aloysius talked with me in detail about how difficult celibacy is for him; he longs for and misses having any sexual expression in his life and has come to accept that the celibate life will for him be a lifelong struggle. He assumed that celibacy was as much a struggle for everyone as it is for him; that was just the way things were.

I asked him if he had ever explored the possibility that he needed not to be celibate at this point in his life. Was he open to explore options? He said that he was not (a sign of addiction) and that celibacy was difficult for everyone. I told him that I knew of many people who felt that their inner process had led them to a place where they were naturally celibate; it did not seem to be an issue for these people. It may not be possible to make a "choice" to be celibate and simply assume that the body and being will follow.

Father Aloysius had made a decision to be celibate and then tried to force his body into compliance. Hence, his life was dominated by the constant struggle to try to remain celibate, and he was obsessed with sexual fantasies that, he felt, were warring against his celibacy. Much of his life was spent obsessively thinking about this problem and trying to control his sexual feelings. When I met him, it was clear that he was living a life of obsession and torment. His "struggle" over his sexuality was occupying much of his waking hours as well as his dream life. Father Aloysius had become a sexual addict. His life had become dominated by his sexual feelings. When I first met him, he was depressed and feeling hopeless. He was fearful of maintaining his celibacy and totally at the service of the struggle. Whatever was going on with his sexuality was the center of his day. He had crossed the line from fantasy to addiction. Instead of having resolved the "struggle" in a way that worked for him, he had become obsessed with it.

It was easy to see that he was in the grip of a progressive disease. His work was suffering; his relationships were suffering (he was so ashamed); his physical health was deteriorating; and he was constantly depressed and anxious. Aloysius saw no way out of his dilemma. He did not believe that a priest could go to SLAA.

He felt trapped in his disease—and he was. Aloysius was a victim of his belief system and saw no way out. His thinking had become progressively confused and distorted, and he was beginning to feel paranoid and suspicious. He had reached the level of despair, and his entire life revolved around his sexual addiction. No amount of confession or "psychologizing" ultimately would help. He needed to confront his addiction. He had lost touch with his spiritual base and the spiritual base of his work. He saw celibacy and sexuality as a dualism and was teetering between the two. Although it was clear to everyone who knew him, it was not clear to Aloysius that he was powerless over his sexual addiction. His life was, indeed, unmanageable.

Masturbation as a Fix

Leslie had started masturbating at a very early age. She had stumbled upon these "good feelings" as a child, and masturbation was a source of comfort for her. Leslie considered her "masturbation time" a time for herself when she could be with herself. She considered herself a sexually liberated woman, and even though she was active with a regular sexual partner, her masturbation was the focus of her sexual life. Leslie rationalized what she was beginning to realize was excessive masturbation by saying that she did not want her sexuality to be dependent upon anyone else; she wanted to be able to "take care of herself" independent of any sexual partner.

However, she had become concerned that her masturbation was getting beyond her control. She was beginning to feel controlled by it. Although she felt good that this sexual obsession was not hurting anyone else, she was becoming aware that it was hurting *her*. She had begun masturbating when she was home alone and had private time. Then she began to explore other possibilities: while she was driving her car, in public toilets, at the movies, at her desk at work. As she talked, it was easy for her and others to see the progression of her disease. She had gone from what could be considered a normal range of sexual activity to taking greater and greater risks with her life. She had had several "close calls" when masturbating while driving, and although they had added to her thrill and excitement, she could see that she had been taking risks with her life. Likewise with her work—she had found herself going to the toilet more and more often during working hours and knew that her work was suffering. She began to "experiment" with what she could "get away with" while sitting at her desk. Again, it was exciting for her to get away with orgasms when others were around, and she could see that she was walking a very fine line. Along with her actual masturbation she began to find herself preoccupied with thoughts of her next opportunity. When she was not masturbating, she was thinking of how and when she could next do it.

Leslie realized that her life was out of control and that masturbation had been the focus of her life. She was turning down dates and time with her friends so she could be "alone." She found herself lying about the "reasons" for being alone; her life was becoming more isolated and progressively constricted. Leslie knew that she was in trouble and sought help. Since many of her friends were active in the local twelve-step community, she shared her story with some of them, and they suggested that she might want to attend SLAA meetings. Leslie started attending SLAA regularly, got a sponsor, started working a twelve-step program around her masturbation, and accepted a plan of abstinence from masturbation.

Initially, she seemed to improve, and then her friends began to notice the old patterns of isolation, dishonesty, "conning" behavior, distractedness, being out of touch with her feelings, and evasiveness. They shared their concerns, and Leslie was quite verbal in her protestations that she was working her program, consulting her sponsor, and abstaining from masturbation. She was "sober" from her sexual addiction, she protested. However, as her friends sat with her and shared how they felt her absence and how she seemed to be just as isolated and withdrawn as before, she began to cry and said that she still felt "crazy" and obsessed. She had not been masturbating; she had been on a wild spree of sex with partners. Leslie had shifted her addiction. It still expressed itself as a sexual addiction, but "the water had found a new path." The "Big Book" of Alcoholics Anonymous says that this disease is cunning, baffling, powerful, and patient. Leslie was experiencing the impact of those words. In abstaining from masturbation, she was able to "con" herself (denial) into believing that she was "sober" in relation to her sexual addiction. She was not sober, she had only switched expression. Some people may switch to another addiction—eating, working, relationships—Leslie had switched to another form of sexual addiction. This form had picked up where the other (masturbation) had left off, and her disease had continued to progress. Leslie was still actively practicing her sexual addiction.

Leslie, however, was lucky. She had a community of friends who were astute about the addictive process *and* the recovery process. They saw her initial improvement and then her quick switch into relapse behavior. They cared about her and knew for themselves the destructiveness of this disease. They shared their concerns with her. She listened. She heard what they were saying, and she is now truly on the road to recovery.

In our discussion of sexual addiction we have now reached what Carnes would call Level One. (Yet we have seen that even Pre-Level One can be severe and even fatal.) Leslie was addicted to masturbation. Yet, she and the others we have discussed are suffering from a sexual addiction and are equally as tormented by this disease as the more dramatic cases we usually think of as sexual addiction. I believe that we are currently at the same stage of understanding sexual addiction as we were when we believed that the typical alcoholic is a street drunk. We know now that the housewife who drinks alone is in as much need of strong recovery as the street drunk or the acting-out alcoholic. The sexual anorexic is as desperate inside as the rapist or the child molester. Her behavior may not be as dangerous to society, *and* it *is* dangerous to her. Now on to other forms of sexual addiction.

Addiction to Lust: Many Wives, Many Lovers, No Peace

Andy was a physician who was in his late fifties when he finally admitted that he had a "lust" addiction. He had come from an alcoholic family and himself had admitted being an alcoholic many years before he admitted his sexual addiction. Although he had quit drinking some time ago, he had never really begun a recovery program and would best be described as "dry," not sober.

⸭ Andy was a strangely attractive man. Looked at objectively, he had a highly developed torso resting on spindly, bowed legs, making his body seem slightly deformed. One experienced him as tall, though he was not, and he exuded a powerful energy best described as sexual in nature. On first encounter, people often felt they were in the presence of a wise person; it was only after a period of time that those who knew him began to feel they had been witness to a truly polished "con." Andy changed spouses, partners, friends, and locales frequently, so his "con" was rarely confronted.

Andy had had many wives, many lovers, and many affairs. He was great at conventions, always the life of the party. Day-to-day living did not suit him well. Andy knew that his life was not working, and he was always open to any new psychological or encounter technique or spiritual approach that came along. He dipped in and out of many new movement fads, but nothing ever seemed to make much difference. In desperation, he left his family, friends, and support system and searched for a guru or spiritual approach that would help him "calm his demons inside." He literally searched all over the world for something that would work for him. Although it appeared he was looking inside, he continued to look outside himself for answers. Never did it occur to him to face his "lust addiction" as addiction.

Eventually, he put himself in a monastery and there felt safe. When he talked with me about his life, he was confounded with his "lust addiction." "I have achieved a certain modicum of peace with my spiritual practice, but I don't dare leave the monastery. Whenever I go into town, I find myself looking lustfully at beautiful women. I become obsessed and confused. My peace and serenity go right out the window." Andy could not handle the outside world. He no longer was acting out his sexual addiction and destroying his relationships with affairs and short-lived liaisons, but in many ways he was still a prisoner to his lust. He never really had the possibility of recovery. In the prime of his life he died in the monastery.

Here we have a person who in his earlier life had married many times, had been involved with numerous lovers, and had many affairs. He always sexualized relationships and knew how to attract and charm women. He had many children, some in wedlock, some not. Some of these children he knew; some he did not. His chief method of relating was through sexuality, and he had few, if any, male friends. Although he had achieved a certain level of competence and recognition in his chosen field, he gained little satisfaction from his achievements. Andy was a lonely man.

Andy's sexual behavior was basically accepted by society, but it was destructive to him and his family. He was a man with a progressive disease who resorted to some rather drastic solutions to try to cope with his addiction. He never did completely break through his denial system or distorted thinking; in a very subtle way, he "protected his supply" until the very end. He died alone without family or friends and truly "escaped intimacy."

His behavior in his early life would probably have been looked at as Level One behavior by Carnes. Later in his life, he was Pre–Level One or not on Carnes's scale, yet he was an active sexual addict and he and his family felt the heavy impact of his disease. He had tried everything that he knew, the "best" that psychology, psychiatry, and spirituality had to offer. Unfortunately, he did not know about sexual addiction at that time. He did not really have the opportunity to face his disease, because it had not been named when he was searching for a solution to his "internal turmoil." He was not one of the lucky ones. Like many others, he never really had a chance.

Since Andy was in so many marriages and relationships, it would be easy to confuse his addiction with a relationship addiction or with a sex *and* relationship addiction. That would be not understanding Andy. Let us look deeper.

Andy had gone to parochial schools and had grown up believing that the only legitimate sex was sex in marriage. He believed that he had to be married or, at least, be in a relationship to have legitimate sex. Hence, he became a "quick relationship" expert. He learned all the techniques for "instant intimacy." He knew how to share feelings (although, as it turned out, he shared the same "feelings" with everyone), listen, and intensively focus on a woman, making her feel she was the center of the universe and nicely hooking into her love and romance and/or relationship addiction. However, with Andy, the goal was to become sexually involved.

Unfortunately, Andy was also a victim of the Madonna-Whore dualism when it came to women. He was always looking for the Madonna (pure virgin), and when he thought he had found her, pressed her into becoming sexual (the only way he knew to relate and the way he got his sexual "fix"). When she succumbed to his sexual expertise (and his *insanity* as he recognized it at some level), she became the Whore in his mind, and he became disappointed and moved on.

Relationships and love and romance really had little to do with what was going on with Andy. As he put it in his later years, his issue was *lust*. He was a sexual addict, and his course of recovery would have to be from sexual addiction. Had his progressive disease been correctly named, he would have had a chance for recovery.

Sexual Addictions and Violence

We now begin to get into what the public would consider sexual addictions: rape, incest, sexual molestation. These forms of sexual addiction must be linked with violence and are most certainly connected with cultural issues.

Carnes gives an excellent description of this level of sexual addiction in *Out of the Shadows*, and I see no reason to repeat what is already an informative discussion. Likewise, Charlotte Eliza

Kasl, in *Woman and Sex Addiction*, does an excellent exploration of women's sexual addiction. Here, I merely want to emphasize some additional perspectives.

Incest and Child Molesting

Incest and child molesting are epidemic in our culture. I never cease to be amazed at their extent and frequency. In my personal experience, the incidence and variety of incest far exceeds any research that we have on the subject and any previous assumptions that I had about its prevalence. I have worked with literally thousands of women as they attempted to work through their experiences of being sexually abused by the very persons that they had a right to trust the most: their fathers, grandfathers, older brothers, mothers, and older sisters. For many years, I held the illusion that only girls were victims of incest or sexual molestation and it was because of their place in the culture. I do believe that female children are often treated like objects (sex objects) and are not viewed as real persons by their molesters. Yet, it was also an important part of my learning when I began to work with men who had not only been molested by the adult males in their lives (which, somehow, I had expected) but also by adult women. This awareness caused me to look at incest and sexual molestation in a broader context and to explore all these issues from the perspective of sexual addiction, which seems to be the paradigm that best fits the information.

What do we know about incest and molestation as sexual addictions? As I have worked with men and women around the issues of incest and sexual molestation, I have noticed several things:

First, the problem is epidemic. I believe that we have no idea whatsoever how common incest and child molesting are. Given that the people who come to my talks and workshops are a biased sample, still, as these issues arise in the groups, there are few females who were *not* sexually abused when they were young and an amazing number of males who were.

Most authorities in the field believe that being molested as a child sets up individuals themselves to be sexual addicts and molesters. If this is true, then it is not surprising that many, many people are self-identifying as sexual addicts.

Second, an appalling number of persons have been orally raped as infants. Until I began working with addiction and moved beyond the verbal therapies into what I call deep living process work, oral rape of infants had not occurred to me, except, perhaps, intellectually. I knew that infants had a built-in sucking reflex and would suck on anything put into their mouths, and I had not imagined the number of men and boys who have put that piece of information together with their sexual addiction. I have worked with an astounding number of people, mostly women, who have a bodily memory of that experience.

Third, sexual addicts, especially those who commit incest, are often pillars of the church and the community. I can recall many painful moments at my intensives when women have uncovered deep, excruciating memories of violent sexual experiences from childhood visited upon them by the adults in their lives.

I remember the first time I sat with a young woman as she painfully and in great terror worked through a "gang rape" by her father and his friends on the kitchen table when she was five. Her pain, terror, and later anger were almost unbearable. Her father was a professional man, a deacon in the church, and he and his friends were having a party one night when she innocently became the object and focus of that party. These were "good people"—or so they seemed. After her uncovering of that important repressed incident, which was the most traumatic of her life, other memories of painful sexual experiences with her father began to emerge.

I know now that this was not an isolated horrible incident. I have sat with more women than I wish to remember who have had the courage to confront and work through incidents of this sort. Most of these women came to consider the perpetrators to be sexual addicts whose lives were out of control and who inflicted their disease on innocent children.

Fourth, sexual addiction, like other addictions, is always destructive. Carnes's levels of addiction move from those addictions that are most socially acceptable to those that are considered illegal, from those that on the surface only affect the addict to those that are violently invasive, and from those with less acting out to those that are purely acting out.

I know that *any* sexual addiction is destructive to the individual addict as well as those around him or her. I also know that this is a progressive, fatal disease that has no regard for age, sex, color, creed, or social status. Anyone can be or can become a sexual addict, and many more people than we realize currently are sexual addicts. Regardless of Carnes's levels, sexual addiction is destructive to the addict and can be fatal.

Fifth, most of our information about sexual addiction has come from persons who sought help. We know little about the sexual addiction, as such, of those who do not choose to get help or recover.

Finally, sexual addiction is well integrated into our culture, and our denial of its existence and our titillation about it contribute to its perpetuation. No exploration of sexual addiction is complete without looking at how it is integrated into a sexually addictive culture and at the purpose it serves in that culture.

Levels of Sexual Addiction

As I said earlier, I believe that Carnes's levels of sexual addiction are good. I would probably expand the levels and add others.[6]

Level One, repressive sexual addiction, includes persons who are obsessed with repressing sexuality—their own and others'—and are totally preoccupied with sex. Included here are such characteristics as frigidity, impotence, sexual righteousness, obsessive sexual purity, nonintegrated celibacy, religious sexual obsession, sexual anorexia, and the treating of others as sexual objects. All of these are forms of sexual addiction and can be just as destructive to the individual and to society as is sexual acting out.

Included at *Level Two*, passive sexual addiction, are obsessive sexual fantasizing, passive pornography (voyeuristic, private), and voyeurism.

Level Three, sexual acting out, includes more acting out such as masturbation, exhibitionism, prostitution, active pornography, "New Age sexual freedom," using one's sexual partner as an object to get a "sexual fix," voyeurism-exhibitionism, public masturbation, sexual telephone calls (sending and receiving), sexual touching fixes (usually public), and autoerotic asphyxia.

I question whether the latter should be Level Three or Level Four. Autoerotic asphyxia is a behavior that has recently come to attention and seems to be related to incidents that were originally thought to be teenage suicides. The idea is to shut off one's oxygen supply, usually by a form of hanging with a rope, while masturbating or having sexual relations. The result is supposed to be a dramatic effect at the point of orgasm or an intensifying of the orgasm. It appears that many more teen suicides than were once suspected are related to this form of sexual acting out.

Level Four, violent sexual behavior, includes individuals involved with child prostitution rings, rape, incest, child molesting, sadomasochistic sex, and other forms of sexual violence. At this level of addiction, the addictive behavior is always directed toward another and is violent in the psychological and/or physical treatment of the self and/or the other. The behavior almost always violates social and ethical norms and usually the law.

These levels are not discrete. They are interactive within each level and between levels. The levels, like the disease, are progressive, although one can be severely addicted at any level.

Although behaviors at any of these levels do not necessarily indicate addiction, if one engages in them, one should stop and carefully assess the possibility of sexual addiction. Sexual addiction at any level is destructive and painful.

What, then, are some of the things we know about sexual addiction?

Sexual addiction is a progressive, fatal disease. Sexual addiction can be just as lethal to the individual and relationships as any chemical or process addiction. In sexual addiction the focus of the addiction is the sexual fix, and little else matters. Persons and relationships are objectified in the service of the addiction, whether it is a repressive sexual addiction or an acting-out sexual addiction. As Carnes says, "Sex is my most important need" is the focus of the addiction.[7] I would say that sexual addicts come to believe that a "sexual fix" is what they can count on in life. Sexuality becomes the core, defining concept in the individual's life and relationships. One needs to consider whether many aspects of the sexual revolution and New Age sexuality may be (not so) subtle ways for sexual addicts to "protect their supply."

In the literature there are confused suggestions that sexual addicts are looking for nurturance and/or a relationship. This has not been my experience. The sexual addiction process will use others' addictions (such as romance or relationship addictions) to meet its needs; I do not find that that process really is looking for intimacy. In fact, I believe that sexual addiction is a way of actively avoiding nurturance and intimacy. Sexual addicts use relationships to get their fix. They are not really interested in love, romance, or relationships; however, frequently, if they pretend they are, they stand a better chance of getting their sexual "fix" under culturally approved circumstances. Because this pattern is so common, I think it is absolutely crucial to separate the concepts of sex addiction, romance addiction, relationship addiction, and addictive relationships.

Sexual addicts, like other addicts, are willing to do whatever they have to do to get their sexual fix; they are willing to be destructive, illegal, or violent. Yet it is important to remember that sexual addiction is a disease that can be treated. These are not bad people doing these bad things. These are sick people acting out of a progressive, fatal disease, and they do, sometimes, do bad things. As I stated earlier, I believe that our knowledge of sexual addiction at present is analogous to our knowledge of alcoholism when we thought the alcoholic was the street drunk and did not understand the range or subtleties of that disease.

It is important to mention here that sexual addiction often does not occur in isolation from other addictions. Sometimes other addictions are used to cover up, justify, rationalize, or nullify sexual addiction.

Relation to Other Addictions

Other Addictions Used to Cover Up

As I stated earlier, I have found more shame around sexual addictions than almost any other addiction. Many people I know who are chemical addicts and sexual addicts readily admit that they would much rather be a "drunk" (their word) than a "pervert" (also their word). There is less cultural judgment against chemical addicts these days.

I have also found that co-dependence has become very popular as a cover-up for other addictions. In fact, any "co" label is more acceptable than an addiction label for some people. I believe that the reason we have confused sexual addiction, romance addiction, and relationship addiction is that the latter two are more acceptable. Moreover, this confusion offers one the cunning possibility of getting off the hook from all three by saying, "This doesn't fit, and this doesn't fit, so therefore, I must not be one." Co-dependents sometimes have difficulty admitting that they are co-dependents *and* sexual addicts, or co-dependents *and* romance addicts, or co-dependents *and* relationship addicts. It is only in facing the *specifics* of the form of our addictive process that we gain the possibility of recovery.

I have seen people use their co-dependence to protect their addictive supply. For example, I heard a woman once say about an incident, "Oh, I must have been into my co-dependence. I was trying to please everybody," when, in fact, she was into her sexual addiction and her greed in relation to her sexual "fix." These addictive processes are indeed tricky.

Other Addictions Used to Justify

The addictions most frequently used to justify sexual addiction are chemical addictions. "I didn't know what I was doing." "I had

had too much to drink." "I am really a drug addict, and drugs affect my ability to control myself and my judgment. It is only under the influence that I do things that conflict with my ethical beliefs."

The chemical use (addiction?) is being used to justify or cover up the sexual addiction. In some cases the chemical addiction is an auxiliary to the sexual addiction; in others, it is vice versa. To begin recovery, it is important to know which is which and to recognize that the addictions support one another.

Other Addictions Used to Rationalize or Nullify

Workaholism is a favorite addiction used to rationalize other addictions. "I work so hard. It's only fair that I would seek a little sexual pleasure." Workaholism justifies acting out.

I have also known sexual addicts who used their workaholism to feel better about their sexual addiction. Regardless of whether they were repressed sexual addicts or acting-out sexual addicts, they used work to expiate their guilt and feel better about themselves. If they just worked hard enough, they would make up for their sexual fantasies, behavior, or acting out. Of course, it never works.

Often overeating is used to avoid a sexual addiction. "If I am not attractive, I won't have to deal with sex." These addictions support one another. The Alcoholics Anonymous "Big Book" says that addictions are cunning, baffling, powerful, and patient. This is certainly exceedingly true for sexual addictions.

The Genesis of Sexual Addiction

What do we know about the genesis of sexual addiction? In some ways, very little. Kasl has found a high incidence of sexual abuse in the histories of women who are sexual addicts.[8] I believe most writers would agree with that observation. Carnes also looks to the family and the effects of an addictive and/or dysfunctional family. I believe that we have to look at the family and beyond to understand sexual addiction. According to Carnes, "Sexual addictions, like all addictions, rest in a complex net of family relationships."⁹ This is true and it is not all that is true. I believe that it is utterly impossible for even a perfectly healthy family system to withstand the influence of the church, the schools, and our culture as a whole. We must look at all of these influences if we are to understand the sexual addictions.

The Role of the Home

In talking about women, Kasl says, "It is difficult for me to separate out the behaviors of a sex addict or co-dependent from a recovering abuse survivor because in my experience, the two are inseparably linked."¹⁰ I agree, and with abuse being so widespread, why are not almost all women sexual addicts? If we lumped together sexual addiction, romance addiction, and relationship addiction, maybe that would include enough of the women in our society to account for the large number of girls who have been sexually abused. [Combining these three addictions (which may combine *and* overlap) is a mistake with respect to the recovery process.] Are all adult female sexual addicts survivors of childhood sexual abuse? I do not know; I do know that many are. Are all adult male sexual addicts survivors of childhood sexual abuse? I do not know; I do know that many are.

Certainly, women and men have learned in their families that their sexuality is one way to make contact, get what they think they want, and exert power. Sexuality is never simple in a sick family. Nothing is.

Sexual addiction is a lack of relationship with the self and with others. Sexual addicts learn in the home to treat the self and others as objects to be manipulated for gratification. When objectified relationships are sexualized, sexual addiction results.

In our society, we have talked so much about dysfunctional families and the role of dysfunctional families in addiction and co-dependence that we have been led into the illusion that there really *are* functional families and that functional families are the norm with which we can compare dysfunctional families. I wonder; is this part of our massive cultural denial system? As long as we can pin addiction on dysfunctional families and make them the primary *cause* of sexual addiction, can we then hold onto the illusion of "normal," refuse to look at the role of our institutions (especially church and school), and avoid completely the role of addictive society? I believe we try to do this when we talk about the dysfunctional family as if functional families existed in great numbers.

How many functional families do you know? How many families did you think were functional only to discover that they just had a good public image? How many perfect families have bit the dust as new information about addictions and co-dependency has come into common currency?

I am not saying that there are no functional families. I am just saying that the way we have approached the concept of dysfunction has led us into seeing things in a way that has fed individual and cultural denial. We need to look at this illusion. In just the last few years we have seen Sharon Wegscheider-Cruse's description of roles taken by members of families of alcoholics applied far beyond her original concept to families in which there is no known chemical addiction.[11] We also have seen the concept of the Adult Child of Alcoholics extended far beyond any hint of chemical addiction and be discussed as Adult Children of Dysfunctional Families. We need to accept and see the role of the family in addiction, *and* we need to move beyond that conceptualization as the *cause*.

I believe that our acceptance of the old cause-and-effect thinking has kept us "hooked" into the addictive paradigm. We need to understand family rules and the role of family in the forming of self-image, belief systems, and core beliefs. That understanding is not going to "fix" the situation. It gives us information, that's all. We cannot then provide the "right" situation or reparent and expect to "fix" addiction. Recovery requires that the individual do his or her own recovery work and ultimately, I believe, make a personal paradigm shift. We each have to work through our own experiences in the family, and we must simultaneously look beyond the family. We have learned to be sexual addicts in the home, and we have also learned to be sexual addicts in our institutions.

The Role of the Church

With regard to sex, both the church and the school operate on the repression-obsession dualism and its corollary, the repression–acting-out dualism.

I believe that obsession and repression go together. Those things we are obsessed with and we try to repress become obsessions. Those things that we try to repress usually find their way out (like water seeking a new path), and frequently we act out in ways that are confusing for ourselves and those around us.

The church is notorious for its obsession with and repression of sex. As one of my Catholic friends says, she was taught, "Sex is dirty. Save it for your husband."

I believe that many of our most outspoken leaders of organized religion are themselves sexual addicts. They are so obsessed with sex that they make it impossible for church members to learn about healthy sexuality in the church. Often, the church makes sex *the* most important aspect of a relationship. It is all right to love each other before marriage. It is *not* all right to be sexual before marriage. Many religious people get married in order to have legitimate sex. I am neither attacking nor condoning premarital sex here. That is not the issue. I am saying when an obsessive emphasis is put upon repressing sexuality, the result is often sexual addiction.

Aloysius, the priest whose story was told earlier, was caught in the net of the obsession-repression dualism. Despite his own confusion, he was teaching others about their spirituality and sexuality. I knew a nun who firmly believed that God was dependent upon her celibacy. After she left her order, she discovered that she is a sex addict and is attending SLAA meetings and is on her way on her way to recovery.

I want to emphasize here that it is not just the Catholic arm of the church that is confused about sex and teaching the obsession-repression dualism. In the news media, especially recently, we are frequently told about our religious and political leaders' sexual acting out. Lives and careers are ruined because of sexual addiction that is not named. Because addiction is not named, recovery is not an option. [Men's lives are ruined and the women are exploited!] Repression begets obsession, and obsession begets acting out. However, often, when our spiritual and/or political leaders act out their sexual addiction it is described as an "indiscretion" and they are not seen as sexual addicts needing help to face recovery from a progressive, fatal disease.

When writers talk about the effects of personal and family belief systems on sexual addiction, they are absolutely right that the beliefs that one is unworthy, a victim, and powerless and that others are to be mistrusted are the very basis of addiction. Yet where do families and individuals get these beliefs? They get them from the schools, from the churches, from the society at large. No exploration of sexual addiction would be complete without looking at the role of our society in sexual addiction.

The Role of Our Society

When I was a budding psychotherapist, I did my clinical internship at a large, well-known Eastern metropolitan hospital. When we had "grand rounds," the process usually involved presenting what was considered to be an interesting case to several hundred people. One of my most memorable experiences there was the presentation of the case of a man who had a "breast fixation." (I am sure that he would probably now be diagnosed as having a sexual addiction and would be referred to a twelve-step group.) The man seemed to be sincere when he stated that he was willing to put himself in this rather frightening situation if there was a possibility that he could get help. He was clearly in psychological distress and stated that he was tormented by his "fixation."

The resident presented the case with some history and thoughts and assumptions; then the supervisor commented on the resident's conclusion. The patient was asked to comment, and then the rounds were opened up for questions from the floor. I sat and watched as this poor man was grilled with questions such as "What kind of breasts do you like?" "Could you describe the kind of nipples you prefer in more detail?" and so forth. He tried to answer as earnestly as he could, but as the questions continued, I began to notice that my colleagues were almost drooling as they asked their questions. The professionals in the room had moved far beyond scientific interest. I then realized that most of the "interesting" cases presented in grand rounds were sexual in nature, and I began to wonder just who had the sexual "fixation" (addiction). I now believe that what I was observing was institutionalized sexual addiction. Those who were there to help were "hooked."

A reliable insider once told me that when the National Organization of Women was in its early stages of growth, certain "watchdog" governmental organizations thought it would be better to nip NOW in the bud. The way they went about it was interesting. When NOW members were at their national convention, their husbands were called and told that the members were sleeping with men at the convention. When the husbands did not jump at this "information" because they knew that there were few, if any, men there, they were later informed that their wives were sleeping with *women*. It is interesting that the tactic used was always sexual in nature.

We live in a society that sexualizes everything and objectifies everything. The combination is deadly. We have long known that women, minorities, the young, and the old are often treated like useless objects in this society and that sexual objectifying leads to pornography, rape, incest, and brutal sexual acting out.

Feminists have long said that battering and rape are political as well as personal. There is no question this is true. Since the Addictive Society and what I have called in an earlier book the White Male System are the same thing, males are much more integrated into the addictiveness of the society, especially sexual addiction, since males tend to sexualize the universe. However, we must remember that addictive patterns are a learned disease, and both men and women are affected.

We women have also been affected by the Addictive System, and to the extent we practice our diseases of addiction we have bought into it. Our only freedom comes from facing our addictive process and beginning personal recovery. Every minority group or movement has believed that they are the only victims or the only significant victims or the most mistreated victims of the society. That kind of thinking *is* part of the addictive system and keeps us separated and embedded in the addictive process. *Our victimization is real, and* so is that of others. Our recovery as a group requires that we give up our terminal uniqueness and see our uniqueness *and* our commonality.

We must remember that addiction is ours. We have learned it in our families, our institutions, and our society, and it is ours. If we learned it, we can unlearn it. If we learned it, it is *not* who we are. Recovery is also ours. From recovery, we regain our personal freedom and begin to separate ourselves from our addictive society.

Violent sexual addiction has usually targeted as victims those who are helpless and disenfranchised: women, minorities, and children, those who do not hold power in the society.

MacNamara and Sagarin, in *Sex, Crime, and the Law*, state that "Most [rape] arrests are of males of low social economic status."[12] The more we learn about sexual addiction, the more we discover about the more subtle and hidden violent acting out in "proper families," the more we must see that sexual addiction affects everyone in the society.

When we think about recovery from sexual addiction in individuals, in families, in our institutions, and in our society, we must face some important implications.

The Effects of Sexual Addiction on the Society

Along with an increase in sexually violent crime, we have seen increases in the sale of pornographic materials and in child prostitution. Sexual addiction can be profitable. I have talked with people whose children have been "stolen" and done some research on child prostitution rings. Why is so little being done about this kind of crime? The parents of stolen children have had to organize themselves and demand the police use technology already in place. In fact, a few years ago, there was no mechanism to trace a stolen child but there was a sophisticated national network to trace a stolen fur coat! We have integrated sexual addiction into our society. Otherwise, how could child prostitution rings flourish undetected? I am reminded of the stories of so many of the German people I know who kept saying, "I just didn't know death camps were happening!" Our addictions keep us so busy and so self-centered that we "just don't know" things are happening. We become inured to what is going on around us. When something is integrated into the society, we just do not see it. It seems "normal" to us, and it *is* in an addictive society.

Sexual addiction removes us from the possibility of intimacy with ourselves and with others. Any addiction prevents intimacy with ourselves. Carnes says, "Addiction is a relationship—a pathological relationship in which sexual obsession replaces people."[13] However, I do not believe that *any* addiction is a relationship. In fact, addiction is the antithesis of a relationship. It is impossible for an addict to have a relationship with the self or anyone else. Addictions make us zombies, and as zombies we are more malleable and controllable. Sexual addiction is so hidden and so well integrated into our society that it has historically remained untreated and hence kept many people more manipulable. Sexual addiction feeds on guilt and shame and results in controllability. It can be used institutionally to intimidate and control the guilty as well as to intimidate and control the threatened.

Sexual addiction confuses and demoralizes a society. Throughout history societies that are in decline have evidenced sexual addiction. When we cannot handle something as basic as sexuality we are in deep trouble.

Sexuality and spirituality are aspects of the human being that are most focused upon and controlled by the system. These are both fundamental aspects of the human organism. They are also areas of human existence over which the system seems to exert the most control. I find this curious. What would happen if people (especially women, who are the most controlled) were in touch with their sexuality and living out of their true spiritual selves? Why has the organized spirituality of our society, the church, set up an obsession-repression dualism with respect to sex? How are spirituality and sexuality linked?

We must also look at the way societal sexual obsession-addiction is used to control basic functions of the society such as mating and the formation of families. We must see the link between societal sexual addiction and incest and child molesting and must see that we cannot deal with these issues purely on a political level. We need to see that maybe even the political process as we know it is a form of addiction.

Another area where the effects of sexual addiction can be seen as integrated into the society and affecting the individual, institutions, and the societal structure as a whole is that of advertising. We need to see how sexual addiction feeds into advertising and how advertising in turn feeds into sexual addiction.

The Probable Cultural Effects of Recovery

What are the probable effects if we face individual and societal addiction? Advertising, for example, will have to change, and that change could have tremendous economic implications. Can we even imagine what nonsexualized ads would look like?

If individuals begin to deal with their sexual addiction, they will begin to be open to the possibility of intimacy with themselves and others. If they are more intimate with themselves and others, they will be less vulnerable to manipulation and control, especially through shame and guilt.

If individuals recover from their personal sexual addiction, they will be less blind to and less likely to participate in the cultural practices of sexual addiction such as pornography and sexualized religion. What does this mean for the culture?

If we begin to see much of what we have formerly diagnosed as psychopathy or sociopathy as addiction and begin to treat it as such, what will happen to the fields of psychiatry, psychology, and social work?

If the church heals from its obsession-repression dualism about sexuality and ceases to put so much of its energy into that dualism, what might it focus upon? Spirituality, perhaps?

We have not even touched upon many of the possible positive (even revolutionary) repercussions of recovery from addictions, especially recovery from sexual addiction. Are we ready for recovery as individuals and as a society? I hope so.

2. Romance Addiction

The concept of romance addiction has been confused with sexual addiction and relationship addiction. As I stated earlier, it is necessary to separate love and romance addiction from the other two for several reasons. First, if a person is a love and romance addict and is trying to work a recovery program around sexual addiction, the program will not be focusing on the core addiction and will not be effective.

Second, confusing these three addictions offers the possibility of supporting the denial system of the addict. It is very easy to say, "I am not a sex addict, so this information does not apply to me."

Third, if we continue to confuse these addictions with one another we will not develop the information and understanding about each specific addiction that we need to allow each to get proper recognition and treatment. We will, in other words, remain at a stage analogous to treating addictions to drugs and alcohol as the same.

Any addiction has elements in common with all other addictions, and any addiction also has its own specific issues and problems that need to be treated specifically. Romance addiction is not the same as sexual addiction. In fact, sexual addiction may well not have any romance in it at all. "Love" and romance addiction also differs from relationship addiction. Relationship addicts do not necessarily care about love or romance (or sex). Love and romance addicts get their buzz, their fix, from "love" and romance, not from sex, not from relationships.

I have used the term *love and romance addiction* up to this point because so much of the current literature about these addictions talks about love, sex, romance, and relationship addictions interchangeably. For the purpose of my discussion here, I want to drop the word *love* for an important reason: I believe that *no interpersonal or pseudo-relationship addiction has anything to do with love*. These addictions may have something to do with the *illusion* of love, and they have nothing to do with true loving and, in fact, are ways of avoiding love and intimacy. Hence, I will speak here only of *romance addiction*.

The romance addict is in love with the *idea* of romance. The romance addict does not really care about the other person. The romance addict is also an expert in illusion, in fact, lives in illusion. For the romance addict, the belief that "some day my prince (or princess) will come" is not a fantasy. It is a real expectation. Romance addicts can also be addicted to causes and romantic (sometimes childishly "innocent") situations.

Characteristics of Romance Addiction

Romance addicts exhibit all the characteristics of any other addict. They have the same distorted view of reality as other addicts. Their thinking processes become confused and insane. They are so focused upon make-believe that reality seems not to exist.

Romance addicts are as dishonest as other addicts. They give a sexual or relationship "come-on" and are really looking for neither. They are looking for the "buzz" and "risk" of the new romance or romantic experience. Candlelight, flowers, romantic settings, and faraway places are the stuff of romance addiction. Romance addicts are much more concerned with the setting than the other person. In fact, romance addicts can practice their disease even without a pseudo-relationship; a person who moves from one "cause" to another may also be a romance addict.

The romance addict uses form as a "fix." If the situation is romantic and dreamlike, then everything must be all right. Romance addicts are talented in movielike settings, with background music, dim lights, *and* illusion. They have learned about the feelings in relationships from movies and popular songs, and they continue to search for those feelings. Romance addiction often keeps one in the future, keeps one from being present to oneself.

Denial is an important part of romance addiction. The real world must never impinge upon the fantasy. It is amazing how strong a denial system can be, holding up through years of disappointing romantic encounters, the addict still demanding that relationships be like fairy tales. Vagueness also plays an important role in romance addiction; it keeps one from making a commitment to oneself and where one is.

Like other addicts, romance addicts have very low self-esteem. They are always failures at their most treasured illusions and believe they could attract a true prince (or princess) if only they were more perfect. Romance addicts loved Prince Charles and Princess Di's wedding. Yet in their own lives, when the prince/princess illusion wears off, there is nothing there.

In the lives of romance addicts, the superficial appearance is the whole thing. Romance addicts do not want to *know* their potential mates. They want to *look good with them*. Male romance addicts want to "have a beautiful woman on their arm." Female romance addicts imagine the tall, handsome stranger—and it is important that he *remain* a stranger.

Romance addicts are experts at instant intimacy. "Our eyes met for the first time, and I knew it was love." "This was the person I had been looking for all my life." (Next week it may be someone else.) They are afraid of real intimacy and, like other addicts, avoid it through their disease.

Romance addiction is also mood altering. One can get "high" from a song, a setting, a memory, an illusion, or a cause. In this society, we are bombarded with fixes for romance addicts, and all these fixes are mood altering for them. Woody Allen's movie *The Purple Rose of Cairo* is about a romance addict. No matter what romance addicts have, it is never enough and it is never as good as the illusion.

Like all other addictions, romance addiction is progressive. Romance addicts spend more and more time in their illusions. and remove themselves further and further from all aspects of their lives, their families, their work, their relationships, and themselves. It takes more to get the same fix.

Some may find it difficult to take romance addiction seriously, yet it is progressive and can be fatal to body, mind, and spirit. Romance addicts will sometimes seek their fix in situations that can be dangerous. They often will use sex as a vehicle for their addiction, even when they have little or no interest in sex. They do not get their high from sex; however, because they use sex as a vehicle they can get themselves in dangerous, even fatal situations. Of course, being distracted by romance fantasies (or any other kind) can be fatal while driving or when one is engaged in any number of other activities, not to mention the eroding aspects of loss of self-esteem, failed relationships, and a life of illusion.

Romance addicts also evidence a loss of spirituality and a breakdown of their own personal morality. They move progressively away from reality, truth, and normal social mores and behaviors in the service of their addiction. Romance addicts can be home wreckers and teasers with little regard for others' needs or feelings.

We see in romance addicts all the same characteristics we see in other addictions. Romance addiction is one aspect of an underlying addictive process and has all the characteristics of addiction; that is, romance addicts become progressively dishonest, self-centered, blocked in their feelings, isolated, fearful, confused, dualistic, controlling, perfectionistic, blinded to their disease (denial), insane, blaming, and dysfunctional. It is important to remember that this is not who romance addicts are, this is their disease.

We have had many books recently like *Women Who Love Too Much* and *Men Who Hate Women and the Women Who Love Them*. These books have offered many women the opportunity to identify themselves and label their experience. This is always the first step in recovery. When we have the "aha" experience of "That's it," we can start the road to recovery. The more finely we can distinguish what is really going on the better chance we have. Women (and men) may look like sex addicts or relationship addicts when they really are romance addicts. They may look like co-dependents and/or co-addicts when they really are romance addicts. I believe that the distinction is important chiefly because until an addiction can be identified recovery cannot begin.

Range of Romance Addiction

So little has been written on romance addiction as such that we have few points of reference in discussing it. Romance addicts, like sexual addicts, take the most sacred and vulnerable aspects of human interactions and feed their addiction. Romance addiction may not be taken as seriously as sexual addiction because societal ramifications are not as obvious, and it does not have the same kind of violence attached to it. However, for the romance addict, this is a serious, progressive disease that is personally and interpersonally painful.

Romance addicts are obsessed with the *accoutrements* of relationships, *not* relationships. They are always waiting for the partner of their dreams to appear. Fantasied relationships are almost always with pedestal figures or persons who are unattainable. Affairs abound with romance addicts, and when they are married, they are always critical of the spouse, who cannot provide the romantic fix. It is impossible for romance addicts to form a happy, committed relationship. They, like other addicts, are terrified of intimacy; other people are just objects to provide their fix.

It is important to remember that not all romance addiction is played out in relationships. Romance addicts can also play out their disease in adventures or causes. The important element is the thrill of the fix.

It is important here to remember that I am describing individuals with a progressive disease that can be fatal. The behaviors described are not who romance addicts are. They have learned the behaviors; the behaviors are the addictive disease.

Level One

Level One romance addicts live in fantasy. Much of their time is spent in romantic fantasies, and they usually never act out their fantasies. They cross over the line of addiction when their fantasies become their focus of life and they are powerless over them. When romance fantasies begin to make a person's life unmanageable, that person has become a romance addict.

Level Two

Level Two romance addicts begin to act out their fantasies. They begin to have affairs, liaisons, and multiple marriages. Their addiction more obviously begins to affect others. At this level, there is more time and energy spent in illusion, and reality testing is showing some slippage. If married, they try to make their spouses and children fit into their fantasy world with little or no regard for who they really are. At this level, romance addicts have more impact on the world around them. Their morality and connection with their spirituality is slipping.

Level Three

As in all other addictions, as the disease progresses, it takes more intensity to provide the "fix." Romance addicts at Level Three need the thrill. They put themselves in sexual situations that could be dangerous. They are not interested in the sex; they are looking for the romantic thrill. Romantic addicts at this level will push to go to faraway places and have romantic liaisons with strangers, often putting their lives in danger.

At this level the addict has no regard for societal mores and accepted behavior. If families are destroyed, children are abandoned, others are hurt, it really does not matter; romance addicts want and will get their fix. Some romance addicts may even try to precipitate violence for excitement and will probably have found someone whose disease fits theirs. It is only in facing their disease and seeing the disease in the other that they can regain their personal power and their health. When these romance addicts hold on to "victim," they continue to be victimized. We must remember that this is a role they have learned from family, church, institutions, and society; it is not who they are.

Stories of Romance Addicts

Living in Romantic Fantasies

Louise was a worker in the church. She had seen herself as rather plain as a child and felt comfortable entering a service profession when she was quite young. She prepared herself for a life of service and was quite outspoken and courageous in her battles for the poor in a large inner city.

She saw herself as a crusader and sometimes even a Joan of Arc for the poor. She was not an easy person to live with and could be quite demanding and controlling in her righteousness. As she entered her late thirties and early forties, her romantic fantasies about saving the world began to dim, and she decided she "wanted a man." She was very inexperienced with men and so desperate to fulfill her fantasies that she went about "finding a man" with the same dedication she had shown in defending the poor.

Whenever any man was nice to her or gave her any special attention, she immediately entered into a romantic fantasy affair with him. (This, of course, had little or nothing to do with who or what he was or what he was feeling or thinking.) She then spent much of her waking hours fantasizing about their "romance" and imagining clandestine meetings in "forbidden" places (like the vestry of the church), stolen kisses, and furtive touches. Sex or relationship were not really important.

She would make telephone contact using almost any excuse and then embellish and overinterpret what was said. She would then begin to get angry when her "fantasy lover" did not initiate contact and would "blast" him when they happened to meet. Much of her life was being lived on a fantasy level.

She decided to leave church work and "live a more normal life." She openly stated that she had decided that she wanted a man. She did not want a relationship with a *specific* man; she wanted a man. Her experiences with men were almost exclusively on the fantasy level, and when she met a man, she doggedly tried to force him into her fantasies. When the man did not cooperate, she felt personally wounded and betrayed. She spent more and more time reading romance novels and bought a VCR so that she could record her soap operas while she was at work and watch them late at night.

Every man she met was a potential romantic lover. She had little regard for his marital or relationship status. As she saw herself losing her moral values, she began to get frightened. She sought help, began to define herself as a sexual addict, and started attending SLAA meetings, but this did not seem effective. In fact, defining herself as a sex addict subtly offered her an opportunity to protect her supply. She knew, deep down, that she was not a sex addict. Working on her sexual addiction allowed her primary addiction to continue untouched. Louise was a romance addict; she only used sex to fulfill her romantic fantasies. She thought that she could *make* her world what she wanted and felt personally attacked and like a failure when she could not. Louise began to get progressively depressed and controlling. She felt terrible about herself and began to complain that she was not pretty enough, no one liked her, and she would never get what she wanted. Her romance fantasies had become an addiction for her, and she was showing signs of a progressive disease.

She was setting up her romantic fantasies in such a way that they could never possibly be met and was removing herself further and further from reality. Her belief system was that of an addict, and she felt unworthy and unhappy. She had entered the downward spiral of addiction. Unfortunately, she had focused on recovery from an addiction she does not have, leaving her primary addiction intact. It is only when we name the specific addictive process that we can begin our recovery.

Pursuing Romance

Richard is an attractive man in his mid-fifties. He is a dry alcoholic, very much a New Age man, and describes himself as a very eligible bachelor (divorced bachelor, that is). He was formerly a business executive and discovered sexual freedom about the same time he discovered health foods, crystals, and some of the newer psychological techniques.

He is interesting, well read, very chivalrous, and charming to be around. Women see him as living proof that "there are some good men left," and he has never wanted for female companionship or sexual partners.

Richard was divorced several years ago and has a polite, if distant, relationship with his ex-wife and children. He is involved in various "New Age" activities and is considered a "man about town" in the city where he lives. Richard can completely charm women and make each one feel she is the center of the universe (for the moment). When several women are present, he always spreads himself around and is subtly most attentive to the one he perceives as having the most status. He has studied various psychological techniques and astutely uses them to charm the women in his life. Women are thrilled by his little notes, his flowers, and his thoughtfulness.

In spite of all the women in his life (each one feeling "special"), he has been involved in an ongoing relationship with a woman in another state who hoped to marry him. Because of "circumstances" in his life and hers, it has been impossible for them to marry or be together, but they have had "this relationship."

He is open with other women about "this relationship," yet most women feel that he is really involved with them. He is almost never without a sexual partner, but his "relationship" does not know about them. "I don't think she should have to deal with the painful details," he says; meanwhile, he has encouraged her to get her sexual needs met. He would understand. She believed that they were in a committed relationship.

Richard openly admits that this was the best relationship he had ever had. He loved her more than any woman he had had in his life; he just did not think they should tie each other down. The closer the time came when they could logistically get together, the more uncomfortable he was with the relationship. So, he set it up so *she* broke it off. Romance addicts do not want to be held responsible for the termination of a relationship, so they always set it up so their partner terminates the relationship— they may have affairs or just start "picking at" the other person.

On the surface Richard might look like a sex or relationship addict. He is constantly sleeping with one or more women, and he is in and out of many "relationships." However, on another level, neither sex nor relationships are important to him. He uses both to support his romantic illusions and his romance addiction.

Although he is constantly sexually active, it is questionable whether Richard even enjoys sex that much. In pursuit of romance, sex is really boring. When he is being honest, he talks about having to "service" women and about resenting waking up and having a woman there who might want to be sexual. He'd rather have the time to himself.

Richard also is not very interested in relationships. It is important that the woman with him be beautiful, important, or famous, but he really does not want to "relate" to her. He has no interest in ongoing close relationships. He loves the feel of being charming and seductive, of having candlelight and flowers, of escaping to romantic settings. He is great at conventions and meetings. However, on a day-to-day basis, he would rather have himself and his space to himself.

Richard is a romance addict. He is so hooked on the romantic quest that he would not let himself commit to a woman he believed he really loved. Like a bee he flits from flower to flower tasting the honey, but he does not want to live through the stages of the flower.

He lives for the romantic moment. This romantic moment does not necessarily have to involve a woman, though it is often heightened if it does. The romantic moment can be almost any experience that would be *considered* romantic—swimming under a waterfall on an exotic island, feasting with natives under the palms, riding a camel at the pyramids, or floating in a gondola in Venice. The romance addict uses anything that is considered romantic by the society as a romantic fix.

Because the focus is on the fix, the addict often misses the experience itself. The romance addict is so busy saying "look at me! I am swimming naked under a waterfall with a beautiful woman," that he misses the experience completely. The *illusion* of the experience is much more important than the experience itself. Of course, it is also important to talk about these "experiences" after one has them. In fact, talking about them is as important or more important than having them. The woman (or man) is only part of the setting that completes the experience. The other person becomes just another stage prop for the fantasy.

Although Richard's life looks like the bachelor's dream, he has a progressive addiction. One might say that he has shifted from the illusion of alcohol to the illusion of romance addiction. He has caused to be terminated "the best relationship he ever had." He never lacks for partners, but as he says, he "does not really have anyone to share life with." He, like other addicts, finds himself putting himself in more and more dangerous and extravagant situations to get his thrill.

One might say, "What's so wrong with Richard? It sounds like a pretty good life to me." In many ways it is. Certainly it is like the Hugh Hefner dream. When women take his attentiveness and stroking seriously and think they have a relationship with him, he just says, "It's their problem. I never misled them." He did and he didn't.

Richard is not raping anyone; he is not molesting children. So what's the problem? He fits well with women who have sexual addictions or relationshp addictions—at least initially. But he just wants the thrill, the new experience.

Unfortunately, Richard is lonely and Richard is depressed. He is using his romantic "fixes" to avoid himself and his own feelings. He is using his romantic "fixes" the same way he used alcohol. It was not until he realized rather dramatically that alcohol was killing him that he stopped drinking. Where will his romance addiction lead? He does not feel powerless over it now. What will it take to make him face it?

Fantasies of the Unattainable

Mary was a successful businesswoman. She had put in many long, hard hours to get where she was, and she was a competent, respected executive. Some time ago, Mary had realized that she was a workaholic and had began working a twelve-step program around her workaholism. Mary was attractive, vivacious, and energetic, and most people liked her. In moments of reflection, Mary feared that her workaholism had robbed her of the possibility of marriage and a family, and then she would realize that she was not really sure she wanted marriage and a family.

As Mary began her recovery, she began to be aware of feelings and memories that she had repressed and that she had used her workaholism to avoid knowing and feeling. As these feelings and memories emerged, Mary realized that she was an incest survivor. This came as a shock, since before her recovery she had had no conscious awareness of it. As she worked through her incest issues, she became aware that the fact that she was an incest victim shed a lot of light on her behavior as an adult. She had always been somewhat fearful of men while at the same time feeling that she needed them. She felt subtle underlying anger at men, which was increased when she felt she needed them.

During her early twenties, Mary had been very active sexually and had had many affairs, most of them with married men. None had been very serious relationships, and she now believes that this sexual acting out was related to her incest issues. As she had worked through her incest trauma and her workaholism, she became concerned that she was a sexual addict and began working a Sex and Love Addicts Anonymous program. Throughout Mary's life she had spent a lot of her time in romantic fantasies. She always imagined herself having affairs with romantic leading men; Robert Redford was her favorite.

As she has worked with the SLAA twelve-step program, she has felt vaguely that this program just did not quite fit. She now sees that as she has worked through her incest issues, she is not acting out sexually and no longer seems to be obsessed with sex or sexual fantasies. She now believes that her romance addiction is much more of a core addiction and that it initially had a sexual focus because of her incest experiences, in which she learned to sexualize relationships.

Mary realized that the only way she knew to approach relationships was sexually and that though she had used sexual fantasies and sexual acting out they were only a vehicle for her romantic fantasies and obsessions. As she looked at her romance addiction, she began to see several common characteristics. No matter what was going on in her life, she always had a fantasy romantic figure with whom she was relating (Robert Redford was usually on duty). The fantasies were not usually sexual, nor were they really about relationships. They were romantic. The person with whom she was relating was always on a pedestal and unattainable. She always put herself down in relation to these "pedestal people" and felt progressively bad about herself, thus feeding her low self-esteem. Although she was a very attractive woman, she *knew* that she could never attract Robert Redford, and she became more and more depressed. Her fantasies and her resultant depression were affecting other areas of her life. She always compared potential suitors to Redford, and they came up lacking. She always compared her dating experiences with her "experiences" with Redford. She became more isolated and more obsessed. No real-life relationship could match her romantic fantasies. She became progressively dishonest about how she was spending her time and noticed that her work was slipping. Since she had experience in twelve-step programs, she began to work a program around romance addiction. This seemed to fit for her.

Mary now feels that her "sexual addiction" was really a romance addiction that she covered up by confusing it with a sexual addiction. She did not do this deliberately. Her romance addiction just had not been named by herself or others. Of course, her disease was playing with the possibility that if she just worked on her sexual addiction and maintained abstinence from that she would not have to give up her romantic fantasy life. As we know, most addicts will do anything to protect their supply.

Mary is relieved to have named what she believes is her "core" addiction (we'll see), and she is starting a recovery program. She has been full of "aha's" since she named herself as a romance addict.

Searching for Perfection

Peter was tall, handsome, and very dashing. In fact, he was quite a peacock. His body was lean and athletic and, since he ran regularly, beautifully tanned. He was very proud of his body, and he strutted rather than walked.

Peter was a master of the cosmetic. It was the surface that counted with him, although he loudly protested that he was looking for a deep, meaningful relationship. His favorite phrase was: "I feel so good when I have a fantastically beautiful woman on my arm." When he insisted upon having an "open marriage," Peter and his wife of many years, Evelyn, divorced, though he believed he loved her deeply. Initially Evelyn had agreed to try out an open marriage. She then had reluctantly resorted to divorce when she realized that she wanted a stable, committed marriage with someone she loved, which she now has. Peter and Evelyn had several children, and the divorce was traumatic for all of them. But Peter needed to have more women in his life (he needed to feed his romance addiction!).

For Peter, the most important thing about a woman was how she looked and how they looked *together*. "The perfect couple" was a favorite romantic fantasy. He wanted his woman to be well made-up and well coiffed. In fact, he would have preferred it if the woman in his life woke up with her hair done and in full makeup each morning. She needed to fit the stereotype of the beautiful woman at all times, even in bed!

Although Peter was very seductive and had had many affairs, he was basically sexually phobic. He found women too demanding sexually and did not really enjoy sex. Often he approached sex as a task to be completed. He had fantasies about sex and the perfect orgasm, but his experiences never quite matched his fantasies. Down deep, he really believed that sex is a nasty business, messy and perhaps even unclean. He would bathe copiously before and after sex and demand the same of his partners.

Peter continually talked about "cosmic mates," and he dreamed of going to exotic places with them. He had a clear picture of what he wanted in a woman. She had to be as beautiful as a movie star, a professional woman, well read, well traveled, strong and powerful (to be an equal to him), athletic and energetic, warm and soft and nurturing. She had to be able to take care of herself and him and not be dependent upon him. At the same time, she had to make him feel powerful and be careful not threaten his masculinity. He would like a woman who was financially independent so she would not be a drain on him, but he did not want to feel inferior to her (he had little money of his own). Peter was born in the South, and the girl of his dreams seemed to be a combination of Jane Fonda and a Southern belle. So far, he had not met a woman to meet these requirements, and when last I heard, he was still looking.

Peter did not think that his criteria for a woman were unrealistic, and he was confounded that he had not yet found her. When the women with whom he was involved did not fit his demands, he became critical, picky, and verbally abusive, blaming them for the relationship's not working. He was quite psychologically astute, and his tactics of psychological warfare were very impressive. He could reduce even the most competent woman to a puddle of mush in a matter of seconds. Women left a relationship with him feeling physically and emotionally battered and with little or no self-esteem. No matter what they did, it was never right, never enough. *They* were never enough. The woman was always the one to break off the relationship. He would never take the responsibility for the relationship in any way.

Peter was often unhappy and depressed. He felt hopeless about his life; he was never "enough" for himself either. He would have black moods of self-castigation and then he would turn his violence on others. He was monumental in his despair when it hit him.

When he was almost fifty, Peter got one of his "imperfect" women pregnant and reluctantly married her. He romantically decided to try fatherhood a second time. Instead of posturing with the perfect mate, he now found himself forming portraits of the "perfect family" in his mind. And so it continues to the next generation.

Peter shows many of the traits of a romance addict. His life centers around romantic fantasies. Reality is a bother. He uses his fantasies to avoid intimacy while pretending that intimacy is what he wants. He is totally focused on the physical-external and believes that looks and appearance are the most important aspects of a person or a relationship. His dream relationships are unattainable. He puts women on a pedestal and then puts his energy into knocking them off.

Peter has concomitant addictions. He is so concerned with his body that he exercises constantly and frequently suffers from injuries and other physical problems. He is anorexic and is constantly focused on food, his and his partner's. Peter is also obsessed with money. It takes money to live out fantasies. And he is becoming progressively physically violent. As his frustration increases and the insanity of his addictive thinking gets worse, he has become more verbally and physically violent. His violence often takes the form of provoking others to violence or of very reckless driving as he escapes from a situation he has precipitated. As his disease progresses, his driving has become more reckless, frightening, and dangerous.

Peter's life is not working, and he expects someone else to make it work for him. His romantic fantasies have reached a level of desperation. As his romantic needs become more and more extreme, he needs more and more perfection and romance to get his "fix." When he and others do not "fit his picture," he becomes self-destructive and violent.

Peter has tried therapy. Peter has tried twelve-step programs. Peter has never identified his romance addiction, and he is not recovering.

A Review of the Levels of Romance Addiction

The *Level One* romance addict is the person who practices his or her addiction almost completely in fantasy. The addict at this level lives in romance novels, movies, and soap operas. Romance addicts cross the line of addiction when they become powerless over their fantasies and their fantasies begin to be destructive to their normal life—for example, the mother who cannot attend to her children when her favorite "soap" is on (in a recent incident two children drowned while their mother was watching TV) or the man who spends all of his free time with his nose buried in romance, mystery, or adventure novels. People like these are not available to themselves or their lives. They are avoiding their feelings and relationships with others. Reality is receding from their lives, and they begin to exhibit the characteristics of addiction like dishonesty, self-centeredness, and control.

Level Two romance addicts act out their fantasies. Louise kept her romance addiction focused on "acceptable avenues" when she was a "crusader for the poor." Her fantasies were more private, and the work she did was good for others. However, as her disease progressed, she left work she believed in to follow her addiction. She began to "hunt" for men and try to force real relationships into her fantasy world. Any tentative interaction was interpreted as a romance. Her obsessive, illusionary activity began to invade more and more of her life. Her control issues multiplied by leaps and bounds. Progressively, men were treated as objects to satisfy her romance addiction, and she gradually pulled away from women friends because they could not provide her "fix." Her growing sense of unworthiness and an erosion of her self-esteem were evident to those around her.

Richard would probably also be considered a Level Two romance addict. He is acting out his romance addiction constantly, and as he puts it, "I never harm anyone [except himself, perhaps, or disappointed self-appointed mates], and I give so many women pleasure." Richard is, however, beginning to show the wear and tear of his life-style. It takes a lot of energy to keep in contact with all these women, much less keep them happy. He has little time for himself, and he really is not in contact with himself. He is going to romantic places with romantic women, and he is "hooked" on the experience, frequently missing what is actually happening in the moment. There is no awareness in him that sex can be an activity that enhances intimacy. Intimacy is terrifying. Sex exists only to serve his romance addiction.

For Richard, women are completely objects. He is not concerned with who they are; he is relating only to "what" they are. If they are not beautiful, "with the greatest knockers he has ever seen," they must be rich, famous, important, or influential. Like other romance addicts, he is only interested in the package.

With the possible exception of contracting AIDS, he is not putting his life in danger. Richard is not superficially being harmful to others. He is, however, devoting more and more of his life to his addiction, and since he is not in recovery from his alcoholism or his romance addiction, they do take their toll. He had to reach a near-death point to quit drinking. What will it take to force him to face his romance addiction? Maybe it will be his depression and loneliness. He does not have contact with his most important person, himself.

Level Three romance addicts begin to act out their addiction in such a way that it is harmful to themselves *and* others and may even verge upon or be illegal.

Both Mary and Peter operate on this level. As the disease progresses, it takes more and more excitement to get the "fix." The thrill of the stolen moment or even the potentially violent interaction becomes part of the addiction. Moral deterioration is now clearly in evidence.

Mary had reached a point in her progressive romance addiction at which she had no reservations about being involved with married men even though this behavior clearly was not in keeping with her personal ethics. Since she was a highly paid executive, no one questioned where she was when she disappeared for trysts in the afternoon. She was breaking her own ethics in two important areas of her life, and she simply did not care.

Peter had crossed over the line of violence in his romance addiction. He was rarely physically violent, except to himself in his diet and exercise and to himself and others with his driving, but he was almost always verbally and psychologically violent. His romance addiction and its concomitant fantasies and illusions had become so embedded in his life that most of his time was spent in his obsessive addictive disease. Other aspects of his life, like work, family, friends, or meaningful relationships all had receded into the background. His whole life became centered around the conflict of his relationships; he could turn the most benign situation into a war. One could almost see the relief on his face when a woman entered the battle and thus became another "imperfect" woman.

Peter earned his living writing articles and short books, so much of his time was spent alone. He was a successful writer, so he did not have to devote an inordinate amount of time to his craft. However, this left him with much time to himself and contributed to his isolation and his romantic fantasies. The line between his fantasy world and the realities he set up became more and more blurred. He saw himself as above the law and truly believed he could do what he wanted. His "black moods," as he called them, were increasing, and he vacillated between acting extremely "macho" and very childlike and vulnerable. Peter's life was not working. He had reached the point where his romance addiction was potentially physically dangerous to himself and others.

Level Four is violent romantic behavior. At this level, the behavior of the romantic fantasies has changed from candlelight and roses to violence. Addicts at this level can get their fix only in violent, life-threatening situations. These may include sex and other people or may only mean taking personal risks that are seen as romantic (and life threatening). The romantic thrill at this level can perhaps best be accomplished alone. Like other addicts, the romance addict needs more and more to get the "high." Fantasies and movies are no longer enough. The romance addict needs real (fantasied) life. At this level, the romance addict may have dropped the sexual or relationship "front" and be going straight for the thrill fix. Or what may have started out looking like a relationship addiction now may be clearly the thrill of relating to someone who is really sick and potentially dangerous. The romance addict has crossed over the line of destructiveness. Romance addicts are destructive to themselves and/or others.

Like the levels in sexual addiction, these levels are not discrete. Persons can manifest behaviors on more than one level, and there is a quality of progressiveness as one moves from one level to the next, though an addict at Level One can be just as sick as an addict at Level Four.

Behaviors at any of these levels do not necessarily indicate addiction, but manifesting any of these behaviors should cause one to take a closer look at the possibility of romance addiction.

Since any addiction involves a distortion of reality, romance addiction is a form of insanity, like all other addictions. As the disease progresses, so does the distortion of reality in the service of the disease. The addict looks and acts more and more "insane." Reality is not adequate for romance addicts; they have to distort it to fit the needs of their addiction.

As romance addicts become more enmeshed in their disease, they tend to become progressively hostile and blaming. Others begin to feel the weight of their disease.

"Normal" fantasies take on an element of desperation; casual liaisons have a frantic feel to them. Romance addicts are preoccupied and obsessed with romantic visions and experiences. The obsession with the intoxication of new love moves into the intoxication of the thrill. Romance addicts are drunk on romance, and their addiction is fully as mind altering as any drug or chemical. If one questions the mind-altering aspect of people who have "fallen in love," it is important to remember that romantic love is a mind-altering situation, and what starts out as romantic love can become a progressive, fatal disease.

When we think of romantic love as the entry into romance addiction, it is easier to separate sexual addiction from romance addiction. Though the vehicle may be the same, the focus is different. I do not intend to explore romantic love, and it is necessary to see how romantic love fantasies lead into romance addiction as well as how cultural sexualization leads into sexual addiction. Romance addiction and sexual addiction are not the same. I do not believe that most sexual addicts are looking for romance. And I do not believe that most romance addicts are looking for a sexual fix. The addicts may behave in similar ways, however, and I think it is important to see these addictions as different in order for recovery to begin.

Relation to Other Addictions

Other Addictions Used to Cover Up

Sexual addiction, since our culture is more intrigued by it and focused on it, can be easily confused with romance addiction. Romance addicts often use sex to approach or support their romance addiction when, down deep, they have little or no interest in sex. Both men and women romance addicts see sex as a vehicle to play out their romantic fantasies and a way of engaging the objects of their fantasies. Since they have such low self-esteem, their beliefs about themselves are so negative, and they put their romantic objects on pedestals, they believe they have to offer them something if they want to get their attention. So they use sex. Sex addicts seduce romance addicts with wine, candlelight, music, and flowers. Romance addicts seduce sex addicts with sex. Either way, intimacy is avoided.

Other Addictions Used to Justify

Romance addicts often justify their addiction to romance by loudly protesting that they really do want a deep, meaningful relationship. They delude themselves and others into thinking that their romantic behaviors are only vehicles to establish something meaningful. (Relationship addicts are suckers for this one.)

Chemicals may also be used in the service of the romance addiction. A little wine, a little coke, a little grass all make the romantic high so much more intense.

Other Addictions Used to Rationalize or Nullify

"One must always have a good wine to have a truly romantic experience, mustn't one?" Many other addictions can be used to rationalize the romance addiction and to enhance it. Ads include cigarettes and liquor in romantic settings. Can one be romantic without the accoutrements? And, isn't romance used to avoid intimacy? Isn't the illusion better than reality?

Can one become a money addict in the service of a romance addiction? I believe so. Romantic illusions take a lot of money. Flying in to "surprise" a lover or always bringing a simple, expensive gift takes money. The credit cards begin to groan.

Also, I believe that relationship addiction is often a cover-up for romance addicts. It looks as though they are looking for and hooked on relationship when what they really want is a romance fix. One may even use a romance fix to avoid facing the reality of a marriage in trouble, believing that romance can solve the problems. Like all addictions, romance addictions are tricky.

Genesis of Romance Addiction

Role of the Home

Most romance addicts, like most addicts, come from dysfunctional families. Since we have not isolated romance addiction from sexual and relationship addiction, the current literature confuses the three so that the descriptions of their genesis are necessarily confused as well.

We find a good number of incest survivors among romance addicts. Like incest survivors who become sexual addicts, they tend to sexualize relationships, but the sexualization is in the service of the romantic fix, not the sexual fix.

Romance addicts have also developed a belief system that pictures them as worthless and of little value. Romance fantasies often function as escape from a hostile, frightening, sometimes violent home situation. They also can function as escape from a plain, boring, "perfect" home situation.

Romance addicts often come from homes that are dedicated to "impression management," doing everything they can to make others see them as they want to be seen or as they *think* others want to see them. Romance addicts often come from "phony families." They have been raised as little princesses or princes and expect the world to be their "cast of thousands" to pull off the illusion. Persons who have been raised as "royalty" do an interesting flip-flop between feeling like the royalty of their illusions and a "piece of shit" because they never can fulfill their own and their parents' illusions about themselves. When the world does not help them, they become furious.

Romance addicts have never been prepared for the real world by their families. Sometimes their illusions are to escape the horror of their reality and sometimes they are simply "the stuff that dreams are made of." In impression management homes, the children are always dressed like dolls and are expected to be part of the portrait of a perfect family; often their arrival has disrupted the portrait of a perfect couple. In fact, it is the responsibility of the children in this kind of family to prove that theirs *is* the perfect family, and they devote much of their lives to maintaining this illusion and trying to reproduce the family addiction.

Like all addictions, this family addiction is progressive, and each generation gets worse and has greater difficulty maintaining the illusion. Persons from impression management families are raised to fit well with chemical addicts, sexual addicts, relationship addicts, and other addicts. They are also prone to food addictions, especially anorexia and bulimia. Impression management families have developed a family delusional system of perfection to which they all subscribe. To admit to problems would threaten the family illusion. Until there is some crisis the family denial system remains intact. These families demand that individuals abandon themselves in order to fit the family illusion. Not only are romance addicts out of touch with themselves, they also fear rejection and abandonment when they are not perfect enough for the family illusion. This leads to feelings of unworthiness and "badness." The romantic fantasy can take care of those feelings, at least momentarily.

Romance addicts do not trust that their needs will be met through normal means (because they have not been), so they believe that they have to resort to extraordinary methods to get even the simplest needs for recognition and nurturing met. The healthy part of the person wants nurturing and intimacy; the romance addict part substitutes excitement and romance for those normal human needs.

Since romance addicts also believe that they are not enough no matter what they do, they have to make themselves artificial and set up artificial situations to try to meet their needs. Also, because they believe that if their needs are to be met they will have to orchestrate the scene, they become master conductors. They are skilled manipulators and controllers, thus frequently driving off persons who potentially *could* meet their needs.

It is important that we do not assume that the family system is the only system that shapes beliefs and behaviors. We have to see that family systems are affected by the institutions of the society and the roles and beliefs that we see in the family are taught by the institutions of the culture.

Roles of Institutions

Many institutions support the escape fantasies of romance addiction. The church supports romance addiction in several ways. One is with the emphasis on a "better life" hereafter. This feeds into escapist fantasies and allows people the illusion that they do not have to deal with the here and now and with reality. Certain uses of ritual also support unreality and escape, creating a hypnotic, illusionary effect that we come to associate with spirituality.

Another way the church supports romance addiction is through the image of the purity and saintliness of the women and the men chosen as models to emulate. They are perfection—anything short is unacceptable. To be like them one must escape the tedium of being a real person in a real body. This sets us up in a "con" with ourselves and others, as we look toward a life without any of the woes of living. Churches are also masters at teaching impression management.

Our schools support romance addiction by using certain books, poetry, and fairy tales and by romanticizing history. We are often taught a romantic version of our history. War is an opportunity to become a hero. The people killed in a war are not real; they are just statistics. It is often said that if old men told the truth about war, young men would never go. We do not always hear the truth in school; we learn what will support an addictive society. The family is not the only institution where we learn our belief system.

No discussion of the schools and their contribution to romance addiction would be complete without looking at the role that sports heroes and prom queens play in the formation of romance addicts. The most touted events in high school are often those most based on romantic illusions. These events are often accompanied by dim lights, romantic music, and Cinderella-like costumes. We are well prepared to be or to become romance addicts.

Role of Our Society

An addictive society is one built on illusion. Its building blocks are the illusion of control, the illusion of perfectionism, dishonesty, confusion, insane thinking, and mind-altering experiences and perceptions. Romance addiction is an essential element of such a society. It is important that everything is "not as it seems." An illusionary society must maintain its illusions.

The media are important teachers of illusion. Films, videos, and soap operas teach the techniques and skills of romance addiction. Teenage songs serve as mantras for instant intimacy, love at first sight, and heroic relationships, all in a setting of candlelight and roses. They also teach that love and relationships are tragic and tragedy is romantic.

Advertising on television and in magazines feeds off romance addiction and feeds into romance addiction. Even "normal people" are romanticized in the media. We are bombarded with the accoutrements of romance addiction. Sex and romance are combined in advertising. They sell each other.

No discussion of romance addiction would be complete without taking a look at the cosmetic and plastic surgery industries. Both are built on illusion, the illusion of perfection. What would happen to them if people gave up impression management, took off their masks, and related as who they were? We're talking millions, maybe billions, of dollars here!

The Effects of Romance Addiction on Our Society

One of the main effects of romance addiction upon our society is that it supports the illusionary focus of the society and avoids the necessity to deal with life, others, and the universe as they actually exist. We are always one step removed from reality when we deal with an illusionary *concept* of reality. Hence, individuals are left confused, frightened, and powerless. When the individuals of the society are in that state, they are more amenable to the dictates of a confused system. The two, then, interact destructively.

Romance addiction removes individuals from having to participate in the "dirty work" or the tedium of life. That can be left to those who are not royalty or those who want to do it. Romance addicts can only be involved in important things or crises—not the everyday stuff of living.

In a society based upon illusion, it is very difficult to know the truth. In fact, truth is a threat to an illusionary society. Jesus said, "You shall know the truth, and the truth shall make you free." There is very little freedom in an illusionary society.

Let me be very clear here to state that I am not *blaming* the individual addict or even the illusionary society. I am pointing out how they interact to perpetuate an addictive society.

Romance addiction keeps individuals, hence society, immature. The American culture has often been likened to an adolescent by other countries in the world; romance addiction contributes to that perception. For a romance addict, it is important and necessary to the addiction to remain naive and innocent. In fact, one of their major roadblocks to recovery is the fear of giving up innocence. In the dualistic thinking of the addict, giving up innocence means becoming cynical, and the romance addict does not want that!

Romance addicts and societal romance addiction keep life on the edge of excitement, chaos, and crisis. Romance addicts like excitement. When things get a little dull, create a little war. When there is such estrangement from feelings, one needs a little excitement to know one is alive. Romance can add this excitement. In this process, however, one becomes divorced from the implications of the outcome.

There are entire industries that have been designed around romance addiction. As I said earlier, these industries (entertainment, cosmetics, cosmetic plastic surgery, to name a few) drastically affect the focus of the economy and vice versa.

The Probable Cultural Effects of Recovery

If individuals choose to face and recover from their romance addiction, there will probably be economic repercussions. Movies may change and develop a whole new focus. A clearer line may be drawn between fantasy and reality, with a clear appreciation for fantasy as such. Cosmetics, clothing, and cosmetic plastic surgery would obviously be affected if impression management were to become less prevalent.

We may also see changes in the prevalence of some diseases, like bulimia, anorexia, and depression. If individuals face their romantic addictions, there may be less relapse in other addictions or less willingness to participate in other people's addictions.

As we mature as individuals, there is hope for our maturing as a nation. If living in reality becomes a norm, there can be hope for more mature responsibility in communities and government. Individuals may demand a spirituality that allows for full participation as an adult and less childlike, sheeplike behavior.

As a culture, we just might begin to grow up. We could give up the innocence-cynicism dualism and begin to have the experience of innocence with wisdom in our personal affairs and in our affairs of state. These may seem like romantic notions, and it may seem as though I am myself caught in the grips of romance addiction as I write this, yet having witnessed the miracle of recovery many times, I do not believe that I overestimate the *possibilities* and the probable waves of influence.

Just as we are seeing in the liquor and tobacco industries, I suspect we will see a marshaling of forces in industries based upon romance addiction. Yet I expect that they can demonstrate the same ingenuity with change as they have in the past and can even move into production of products that support healthy beauty and recovery. We have seen the recovery of one individual affect an entire family system. We have seen the recovery of one or more individuals affect entire organizations. The idea of these

waves expanding is not pure fantasy or illusion (I don't think!).
I am not suggesting a cause-and-effect relationship between the
society and the individual romance addict. I am suggesting that
we see that the society has reason to promote romance addiction
and that the romance addict has invested in the perpetuation of
an illusionary society.

3. Relationship Addiction

There are two main types of relationship addiction. In the first, a person is addicted to having a relationship—any relationship, real or fantasied. In the second, a person is addicted to a *particular* relationship with a particular person. In the first type the person is hooked on the *idea*, and in the second type the person is hooked on the person. Some Type II relationship addicts can be out of relationships for long periods of time and be quite comfortable yet immediately get hooked whenever they get into a relationship.

A Type I relationship addict is someone who is addicted to the concept of relationship. Relationship addicts do not have relationships, they have hostages. They relate to their *idea* of a relationship, and the reality of the other person or persons is irrelevant. Both types are willing to sacrifice personal spiritual and moral values to hold on to the illusion of being in a relationship. In fact, in Type I relationship addiction the illusion itself is what provides the fix. For relationship addicts the fantasy or belief that they *have* a relationship is the mood-altering drug. The obsession is with a supposed relationship, not with a person. Carnes's addiction cycle fits well here.[1] For both types we see the following:

Preoccupation: an obsession with a relationship, which has a trancelike, mood-altering facet to it, and total absorption in the relationship.

Ritualization: engaging in behaviors that are related to "establishing a relationship" such as losing weight, becoming beautiful again with new hairstyle, clothes, makeup, and so on. Ritualized "courting" behavior may be included.

Compulsive relationship behavior: establishing *a relationship* as soon as possible, discussing and/or doing "marriage" (one relationship addict had been married ten times by the time she was forty-two), or in other ways *nailing down* the relationship and holding on to it for dear life.

Despair: the awareness that the "fix" is not working and feeling hopeless and powerless related to that awareness.

Characteristics of Relationship Addiction

Type I relationship addicts want *a relationship*. In their disease process, they are little concerned for who or what the other person is. They just want someone. They do not see a relationship as evolving; they do not check to see if backgrounds, value systems, or goals in life match well. Relationship addicts just "go for it."

Relationship addicts are consummate "cons." Since relationship addiction is their focus, they have developed the skills for forming (sick, non-, pseudo-) relationships.

Both Type I and Type II relationship addicts have often developed skills—listening, sharing feelings (though not real, costly ones), being there and paying attention—that are quite seductive and useful. In fact, because of these very skills they use as a subtle con, relationship addicts are difficult to detect (by themselves or others). Relationship addicts have devoured the how-to books on relationships and have practiced the exercises with great dedication, becoming experts in the "techniques" of relationship. In addition, relationship addicts have an "openness" con. They use for manipulation and control skills that appear to be being used to develop a relationship. They "protect their supply" by doing all the "right" things in a relationship. Both types of relationship addicts know and practice the superficial skills of social interaction. They do not know how to be friends or establish true intimacy, but they are skilled at feigning relationship. In their *fear* of intimacy they are much more comfortable with the illusion of intimacy. Type I relationship addicts marry the relationship, not the person.

Both types of relationship addicts are absolutely terrified to be alone, and when no one else is around, they believe they are alone. They therefore must move from one relationship immediately to another. They never take the time to feel the grief of the termination of a relationship and thus carry all their unresolved feelings into the new one.

Relationship addicts, especially Type II, have selective amnesia. In order to maintain or be in a relationship, they selectively forget what it was like last year, last week, or yesterday.

Relationship addicts lie to themselves and others about the personal and familial sacrifices they are making to stay in the relationship. They frequently sacrifice their children's well-being for their fix, thus putting the safety of themselves and their children in jeopardy for the sake of their addiction.

Both types not only sacrifice their own moral and spiritual values, they find themselves spending so much time trying to maintain the relationship that they do not have the time necessary for any spiritual life or personal growth. "Burned out" relationship addicts become progressively deadened by their disease, and any spiritual awareness becomes meaningless to them or just too exhausting.

Relationship addicts are very controlling. They believe that they can *make* relationships happen by sheer force of will; they believe they can make another person love them through sheer tenacity. In this process they become progressively more controlling, defensive, and blaming.

Men who are relationship addicts believe that they cannot survive without a wife, and women relationship addicts believe they have no identity without a husband. Both heterosexual and gay and lesbian relationship addicts *must* have partners. It is absolutely essential to be part of a couple. Persons suffering from this addiction look to the relationship to tell them who they are. They have no concept of establishing an identity *of* their own, *on* their own. They fantasize wanting to be together and hang onto each other even when they need time and space for themselves. Their belief is, "if when you go away I don't feel like I exist, then I must love you"—to paraphrase so many popular songs.

Since relationship addicts have been molded so much by the popular songs of our culture, they believe that suffering and loving are the same. They go together; someone who is not suffering must not be in love.

Relationship addicts share the same characteristics of addiction that we have seen in other addicts. They are just as isolated, dishonest, controlling, manipulative, perfectionistic, self-centered, and so on. Relationship addiction is painful and progressive. One relationship addict I know who was in the chronic stages of the disease said that he was fully as insane and destructive when he was in his relationship addiction as he was just before he went into treatment for drug and alcohol addiction. He noticed the same kind of mind-altering buzz when he was pursuing a relationship as he did when he was drinking.

Relationship addicts are often concerned about or jealous of a partner's previous relationships or marriages. They cannot tolerate the knowledge that the focus of their addiction had a relationship with anyone before them. To be a "true" relationship, it has to exist in a vacuum, suspended in time and space. As the disease progresses the intensity of the jealousy increases. Jealousy probably is not a normal human emotion. It *may* be a normal emotion for a relationship addict in her or his disease, however.

Often because of jealousy or just because they feel so frantic and confused, relationship addicts find themselves snooping and spying in spite of themselves. This behavior often threatens their own morality and belief system, but that morality becomes secondary to the disease.

Relationship addicts are constantly anxious and depressed. Since they have made the relationship the source of their validity, meaning, and security, they *must* hold on to it. Asking the relationship to provide this, of course, is asking it for something it cannot possibly provide. The unconscious or conscious awareness of this reality results in progressively controlling behavior. As relationship addicts become increasingly aware that they cannot control the relationship, they become more and more desperate, often making accusations and precipitating battles, with concomitant feelings of desperation.

Even when they know the relationship is destructive, they will cling to it. As these behaviors become more and more intense, relationship addicts feel crazier and crazier and are not able to trust their own instincts.

Goldie Hawn's character in the movie *Private Benjamin* is a good example of a relationship addict. She was raised to be in a marriage and nothing else. In the movie, Judy Benjamin had no concept of self. Her only goal in life was to be in a marriage in which she would be taken care of. When her second husband died on their wedding day, she had no idea what to do and drifts into joining the army. We then see a person beginning to develop a concept of self and of self-worth. She does fall into a "relationship" with an eligible man and is on the verge of a third marriage. However, this time, since she has a sense of self, she is not willing to feel crazy when she discovers the truth about him, and she walks out. The scenes that show her finding evidence of his sleeping with others and his (I suspect) sexual addiction are classic. He tries to convince her that her suspicions are her craziness, lack of love, lack of understanding, and so forth. I am sure that these scenes are familiar to any relationship addict. She almost buys his manipulations, but then she trusts her perceptions and walks out. A relationship addict would have hung on to the bitter end.

Much of what we have previously described as co-dependence is probably relationship addiction, and many or most co-sex addicts are probably relationship addicts. The focus in co-dependency upon controlling others may well be relationship addiction. We need to separate relationship addiction and co-dependence and "clean up" both concepts.

Range of Relationship Addiction

Again, the literature is sparse on work that separates out sex, romance, and relationship addiction. Yet I do feel that it is important to do that, because each of these addictions has a different "feel" and a different focus and I believe that having more clarity about each will facilitate recovery.

As we learn about addictions, their role in the society, and the path to recovery, the knowledge and experience of all of us who are recovering and working in the field is important. The delineation of levels of relationship addiction that follows comes out of what I have seen.

Level One, Anorexia, includes persons obsessed with relationships; they are obsessed with *avoiding* them. I am not talking about the comfortable "loner" or the person who is not in intimate relationships by choice. I am talking about those who may even think they want relationships, are obsessed with them, and do everything that they can to *avoid* them. The key here with respect to addiction is obsession. This is a person who can appear phobic and frightened. This person feels he or she *should* have relationships, should be part of a couple, and down deep is terrified of that. As these addicts move further into their obsession, they become more and more isolated. This is the kind of person who might never be detected as an addict or might use any number of other addictions (chemical, for example) to cover up this core addiction.

At *Level Two*, the addict spends much of his or her time in fantasied relationships. These differ from romantic fantasies or sexual fantasies in that the focus is rarely on moonlight and roses or on sexual liaison. The fantasy is in being *coupled* with another person. There is little content to the fantasy other than the coupledness, the need for the belief that theirs is *a relationship*. Relationship addicts can have a fantasy relationship with someone they know or do not know, and that person can be completely unaware of it. The line of addiction is crossed when addicts begin to believe in the reality of these fantasies, sculpt their lives around them, let these fantasies interfere with their work, their friends, and their lives, get an addictive "high" from the fantasy relationship, and become confused and withdrawn. In the field of mental health, we have known cases like this, and we have never treated them as relationship addictions. Perhaps we need to do this now that we have more information about the addictive process.

Level Three I call "normal" relationship addiction because I believe this is the level we usually think of when we think of relationship addiction, and because addiction at this level is very common in our society. These are the women and men we read about in *Women Who Love Too Much, Men Who Hate Women and the Women Who Love Them, Looking for Love (In All the Wrong Places),* and in the classic *Love and Addiction.* These are the people who are acting out their relationship addiction *in* relationships. Often addicts at this level have been in many relationships and go from one to the next, but some may just stick with one even though it is not really a relationship. The important thing is to be *in* a relationship, any relationship. When one goes sour, as they almost always do, another is in the bull pen warming up. Addicts at this level marry people they do not even know or like just to be married. There is a frantic quality to their quest for relationships and a terror that is palpable if they think they may be *alone*. People are mere objects for the relationship fix. Addicts will stay in painful, dead, destructive relationships because they must have their fix. Although we have seen more writing about women with this addiction, I have found that just as many men suffer from it.

Level Four includes violence and death. People die from relationship addiction. In a conversation with a director of a pain clinic, I discovered some interesting statistics. People went to that particular clinic when they were in the final stages of cancer or had back pain or other chronic conditions. According to my friend, they could help about 80 percent of the people who came. Of that 80 percent, about the same percentage suffered from what he called spiritual, psychological problems. Of this group, he believed most were in a dead or destructive relationship, and he saw these relationships as the key to the physical problem. Addictive relationships can be fatal, physically, mentally, and spiritually. They just seem to grind a person down.

There are other life-threatening aspects of relationship addiction. Because of the mood-altering, insane, illusionary aspect of relationship addiction, addicts lose contact with the awareness that they have options, and they often stay in situations that are physically dangerous. At this level of the disease, judgment is so impaired and self-esteem is so low that they simply cannot mobilize themselves. They may even *hope* to be killed. In fact, they are frequently suicidal. The disease reaches a level where homicide or suicide are very real possibilities and may seem the only options. The threat of being without the "relationship object" evokes violence of one kind or another. These are the final stages of relationship addiction. Chemical usage frequently occurs at this level. The relationship addiction has reached a level where nothing matters.

Like romance addiction, relationship addiction is difficult to see as fatal. Yet those of us who have been working with it for some time recognize that it follows the same course as any other addiction and is progressive and fatal. Dead relationships can be literally that—dead relationships. I believe that we know much more about addictive relationships than we do about relationship addiction. Relationship addiction leads to addictive relationships; the two are not the same.

Stories of Relationship Addicts

Relationship Anorexia

Tony was in his mid-forties when he discovered that he was a relationship anorexic. He had grown up in an Italian family in an ethnic neighborhood in a large city. He was not terribly interested in relationships and did not date much in high school— even though he thought he *should*—and spent long hours worrying about why he did not. His family expected him to get married, and he assumed he would. He seemed to have no concern for *who* he should marry or *why* he should marry or what kind of relationship would lead to marriage. He felt bewildered about the whole thing while secretly thinking there must be something wrong with him. While he struggled with all this confusion, he ate. Food was a comfort.

Tony asked the first woman who showed any interest in him to marry him, and she did. He had no idea what to do next, so he progressively withdrew and "ate" over the next few years. He was depressed and withdrawn, yet obsessed with having this "relationship." He did nothing to develop a real relationship and was content to be in *a* marriage. After a few years, he decided that he was gay and left the marriage for a relationship with a man. He approached this relationship the same way. They quickly moved in together, he withdrew and ate, and nothing happened. After a few years, they split up, and Tony now lives alone. He has not really let go of this last relationship, nor is he "in" it. It just "kinda hangs around."

In the meantime, Tony has decided that he is an overeater, and he is successfully working an Overeaters Anonymous twelve-step program. He also believes that he is a co-dependent. As we were talking one day, he said, "Do you think there is such a thing as a relationship anorexic?"

"I don't know," I said. "What do you think?"

"I think I am one," he said. "I always have these kinda 'fringe' relationships. I am not really in them, and I can't seem to get out of them." His old "lover" was still around, had followed him to a new city where he had a new job, and Tony was constantly worrying about the "nonrelationship."

"I know how I get when I am in my addictive disease around my eating disorder, and I observe that I have the same thoughts, feelings, distortions, highs, low self-esteem, control, and dishonesty around my avoidance of relationships. I believe I am a relationship anorexic," he said. "I avoid relationships, and I obsess about them all the time. When I am obsessing, I exhibit all the characteristics of my addictive disease."

Fantasy Relationships as Fix

Christine was a fantasy relationship junkie. She had tried several relationships, and they had not "worked." She still believed that she needed to be in a "relationship," but she did not have many prospects. She had tried to turn one casual acquaintance into a relationship and that had not worked, so she had given up. But she had not given up on her relationship addiction.

Christine obsessed about relationships, and when she fantasied about possible partners, she never had sexual or romantic fantasies, she fantasied about being part of a couple. Couples do this. Couples do that. She wanted to be part of a couple.

Since she worked alone, she could spend much of her time in fantasy. She neglected herself and her work for her fantasies. She invented suffering relationships that could fulfill her relationship fantasies. She had come from an alcoholic home and had no role models of relationships that were functional, yet she wanted a relationship. Fantasy relationships seemed safer. She believed that if she was good enough, pretty enough, and understanding enough she would find her man.

Christine was a good listener, and she knew that men wanted to be listened to. She listened carefully and really tried to understand every man she met. Her life was similar to that of the little bird who falls out of the nest in the children's book *Are You My Mother?*² The baby bird goes up to everything it sees and asks, "Are you my mother?" Christine approaches every man she meets with the unspoken question, "Are you my cosmic mate?" She is sure that her cosmic mate exists somewhere—if only she can find him.

Her life totally revolves around her quest for her cosmic mate. She attempts to force everyone she meets into her fantasy. She now has reached a point where all she needs is the fantasy to get the buzz.

Running from One Relationship to the Next

Lon was in trouble again. He was about to be without a "relationship," and he was *frantic*. He had come from an alcoholic family in which his father had periodic nervous breakdowns and his mother was an alcoholic. He had been molested as a child, and it was only now that those memories had begun to emerge.

In his mid-teens, Lon had escaped his home as soon as he could by getting his girlfriend pregnant and marrying her. He left that marriage for a second, third, fourth, and fifth. He was always careful to have another relationship lined up before he left the one he was in. When he left, he either left in a huff after a fight he had (unconsciously) precipitated or he sneaked off when his wife was not around—no good-byes, no regrets. He ran. He ran from one relationship fix to the next. He had been doing this all his life. After five marriages, he became involved with men and repeated his cycle. When it looked as though one relationship was on the rocks, he was on the telephone setting up another "fix." He wasted no time. When he did not have a relationship to go to, he had nothing and was nothing. Anything or anyone would do.

Lon carefully watched other people. He wanted to learn the "techniques" of relationships. He had learned little about relationships in his family of origin, and he believed that if he could just learn the "techniques" he could have what he wanted.

School had not been a high priority for Lon, nor was professional training. So, as he neared fifty, he looked back on the carnage of dead relationships with little savings or plans for his future.

He had expected his relationships to provide him with identity, security (both financial and emotional), information about who he was, and someone to take care of him. He was willing to give anything up to have a relationship, and he had.

Lon had developed such a relationship "con" that no one knew who he really was. When friends got together and shared information after he "ran," no one had the same perceptions. No one knew him. Everyone knew one con or another and thought this was the real Lon. He told each what he or she wanted to hear.

In his last situation, he had developed a broad support system of friends, in and out of the twelve-step community. He had a good sobriety from drugs and alcohol and was a solid "program" person. He seemed to be doing the best he had ever done. Then, when his former lover entered a new relationship, he fell apart.

He was obsessed with his former lover and willing to leave family, friends, job, and support community to go to him. He himself admitted that he felt as crazy as he had when he had gone into treatment for drugs and alcohol. His twelve-step friends became concerned with his addictive behavior, were afraid he might drink again, and did an intervention. At this intervention, he was cold, angry, withdrawn, and vicious. When given the opportunity to face his relationship addiction, he stated that he was not *willing* if it meant giving up his relationship with his ex-lover, and he got ready to run again.

However, his "con" was trickier, his disease had progressed, and he used his con to protect his supply. Although he was not present to himself or others, he tried to act as though he were just fine. His plan was to leave and then go to his ex-lover, but he needed others to believe that was not what he was doing. It was important to him that others did not think he was in his disease.

Unfortunately, when Lon tested his relationship fantasy with the ex-lover, the lover wanted no part of it. Lon had no place to go—no time for regrets, he was immediately on the phone and off to be with another former lover. He's still running and unwilling. His behavior is, indeed, similar to when he was drinking.

It is typical of addicts to give up anything or do anything to protect their supply. Relationship addicts are no different. The supply is the "relationship" fantasied or actual. When the fantasied relationship "broke up" amid screams and tears, he immediately set up something else. There was no time taken to deal with grief or good-byes, no time to explore the validity of his friends' intervention. He is "on the road again." He has robbed himself of the love and support available to him because it did not come in the form of *a* relationship. The skills learned in many years of addiction are being used in the service of his relationship addiction, and even he knows that recovery is only possible if one is *willing*. It is difficult to imagine what his "bottom" will be in this one. In his clearer moments, he states that he believes that his relationship addiction is his core addiction. It is unbelievably tricky because the skills being used in the service of the addiction are pseudo-relationship skills. Separate individuals are easily fooled. It was only when his friends compared notes that they all realized that none of them knew who Lon really is.

Risking Death to Save a Marriage

Barbara had been married for twenty-five years when she made her last suicide attempt; she had been on antidepressants for years and had come to the point of believing that she would either commit suicide or die from the drugs. She had tried various kinds of therapy, had really liked her psychiatrist, and yet nothing seemed to help. She and her husband were devout Catholics, and neither believed in terminating the marriage. In fact, she said that the reason she had not killed herself thus far was because of her beliefs and the rules of the church, not because of herself or her children.

On the surface, it looked like Barbara and Hal had a perfect marriage. They were both active in church and community. He was a successful businessman, and though she was trained as a teacher, she had given it up to marry Hal.

Hal had very clear ideas about who and what he wanted his wife to be, and Barbara did everything she could to find out what he wanted and to be that. She was pretty, slim, intelligent (but not too intelligent), and religious just the way he wanted. Their "otherwise perfect marriage" was only marred by her depression and occasional suicide attempts. Both of them believed there was something wrong with *her*, and both were comfortable with that belief.

One day Barbara's therapist introduced her to the concept of co-dependence. She began reading the literature on co-dependence and discovered herself. She began to attend twelve-step meetings and get better. As she improved, she terminated the antidepressants with her psychiatrist's help and began to feel stronger and stronger. She started to take some graduate courses at the local college and sometimes felt almost happy. She still had bouts of depression and occasional suicidal thoughts, *and* she was doing much better.

Barbara was beginning to see that she would do *anything* for the relationship. Although she had little interest in sex, she dutifully performed whenever her husband wanted her to. As she valued herself more, that began to change. He was not pleased.

She realized that she so fully had tried to be what she thought he wanted that over the years she had completely lost contact with herself. In fact, she felt she *had* no self. She believed that she had already killed her being, and her depression was a result of the loss of her self. It was only her body that survived.

As she began to be more in touch with herself, old feelings and awarenesses emerged. She was an incest survivor, and she began to work through those feelings. Her husband was completely supportive as long as she agreed to have sex with him and not let her recovery change their marriage. As her incest work progressed, she no longer could have sex with him. In anger he moved out, asked for a divorce, and began to see other women.

It was then that she realized she was a relationship addict. She went crazy, was furious, and would do anything to get him back. In great anger she said, "He promised to love me in sickness and in health. He is fine when I'm sick, and now that I'm beginning to get healthy he wants a divorce." Barbara was reaching a point where intimacy might be possible for her. Hal did not want intimacy. Hal wanted sex.

Indeed, he was a sexual addict. Barbara had been willing to give herself up completely for the relationship. Traditional therapy did not help her confront her addiction; she went into treatment for relationship addiction and is now in recovery.

Relationship addiction, like any other addiction, can be fatal. Barbara almost died. She had almost killed herself psychologically, spiritually, and physically. She had reached a point where she was willing to do anything to be the "nonbeing" that her husband required in a marriage, even kill herself. Barbara was lucky; she recognized that relationship addiction was her core addiction, and she is, as she puts it, "fighting her way back from death." Some are not so lucky. Her suicidal depression was a result of her relationship addiction. Treating the depression chemically or "psychotherapeutically" had not helped her because, as she says, "They were treating the wrong disease."

A Review of the Types and Levels of Relationship Addiction

Relationship addiction is one of the most subtle and insidious of all the addictions that we have thus far isolated. There are several reasons for this. One of the most important is that the very skills used to practice the disease—the skills we think will establish intimate relationships—are used in a dishonest, "conning" way. This is disarming. These skills are learned early and deeply integrated into the society. Let me give an example.

One of my friends, an excellent therapist and mother, was recently discussing relationship addiction with me.[2] She zeroed in on an aspect of relationship addiction training that I had not recognized. "You know," she said, "I am very concerned about the development of the 'best-friend' relationship that I see in my daughter and her friends. I see the very same characteristics and processes developing in these kids that I see in relationship addiction in adults." Since most of us see the best-friend phase that kids go through as quite "normal" for a particular stage of life, I was not clear about what my friend was seeing. She said that she saw kids learning all the dysfunctional relationship "skills" that they use in addictive relationships as adults. These "skills" show themselves in jealousy, scarcity beliefs (there's not enough, if my best friend has another friend, there will not be enough for me), needing to be with each other all the time (being "best friends" means we are never separated), control, intrigue, suffering, constant crisis, and dishonesty. "I see these kids building relationships and acting just like the relationship addicts I am treating in my practice," she said. These young teenagers are repeating the models they have learned for relationships and are actually practicing skills for relationship addiction. The models they have around them and the songs that are constantly pounding in their ears are preparing them to be relationship addicts. We constantly hear that we need to be coupled to be complete, yet the models we have all around us are of relationship addicts, not healthy relationships. My friend felt very discouraged with this awareness and keenly observed how completely relationship addiction is integrated into the society.

Both Type I and Type II relationship addiction can occur at any level and show many of the same characteristics mentioned in the earlier descriptions of relationship addiction. Type I relationship addicts are addicted to having a relationship, *any* relationship, and when they have relationships, they have them addictively. Other people are truly objects to them, and the person or the personality has little meaning. They exhibit the same kind of frantic acquisitiveness as we find in a drunk hunting for a drink. Any fix will do. Like radar, they are always scanning the horizon for possibilities.

Type II relationship addicts are more selective in a sense. They attach themselves to a person and must have *that person*. Over time, they are willing to give up themselves, their dreams, their identity, their beliefs, and their meaning to hold on to this specific person. We have come to assume that this is what has to happen to maintain relationships (it's called compromise), and we willingly move into these addictive behaviors to achieve "stable" relationships. This type of behavior is so common in individuals and this type of relationship is so common in our culture that we have come to think of them as "normal." Moreover, since one of the characteristics of addiction is that it is progressive and dulls our senses, we lose our ability to stand back and see the painful absurdity of our behavior. We are hooked. Unfortunately, we are hooked on something that is totally integrated into our society. The other two addictions that I see as being this well integrated into our society are workaholism and addiction to money. If everyone thinks something is normal and good, it is difficult to see it as an addiction—as a disease. We call relationship addiction by various pseudonyms: closeness, commitment, security, loyalty, oneness, devotion, togetherness, and love.

Relationship addicts do not have a lot of support to get well, and they frequently are seen as suffering martyrs that put up with so much. I suspect that a lot of what we initially identified as co-dependence was really relationship addiction—people who were willing to stay in completely destructive relationships because of their addiction and because their self-esteem, perceptions, and personal power had become so battered by the relationship they did not have the strength to leave or to do something differently. I believe that we are doing these persons a disservice by treating them as victims and depriving them of the knowledge that they, too, have a progressive, fatal disease from which they can recover if the disease is named.

In some ways, the levels of relationship addiction are like a progression of the disease; however, people who are sexual anorexics or fantasy relationship addicts can also be in the serious, chronic stages of relationship addiction. Both Tony's and Christine's lives are greatly affected by their addiction, and they exhibit all the characteristics of an addict. Lon and Barbara are in severe chronic stages of their disease. They are willing to sacrifice every aspect of their life, in fact, even their life itself for their fix. They both are hitting bottom, and it may mean death for both of them if they do not confront and recover from their addiction. Barbara is sincerely trying. Lon is not ready for recovery and may have to precipitate even more crisis in his life to be brought to his knees. Looking at the levels of the disease suggested here can, at least, offer us an opportunity tentatively to develop a better understanding of relationship addiction as a serious disease and form of addiction in its own right.

Relation to Other Addictions

Other Addictions Used to Cover Up

Interestingly enough, relationship addicts will use both sexual and romance addiction as a cover-up or way of approaching their fix. As I stated earlier, relationship addicts are rarely really interested in sex or romance but in a relationship fix.

Recently, I received a letter from a self-defined relationship addict. In her letter Jean said:

Three weekends ago I was feeling anxious and uneasy about the day so I prayed about that and decided to lay [sic] down and be quiet for a while. I went into a brief sleep and when I awoke, the words "relationship addiction" came to me. So I stayed with that and realized I was feeling a sense of inadequacy and discontentment with myself. I became aware of the same feeling coming up on weekends, usually when I have a tendency to spend alone time at home.

The weekend after, I just happened to look out my window and saw my old boyfriend run past my window. (He's an avid runner and my apartment is right on the beach.) I wanted to leave myself and follow him. My disease was triggered for me then. For the next week, I was aware of my wanting to have my fix with him—which would usually mean my calling him or seeing if we could get together and, as in the past, this would eventually lead up to sleeping together—at which point I would feel such extreme guilt and reject the relationship completely. I have since told him it is not possible for me to see him, call him, or do things together and that I would appreciate that he wouldn't call me. This recent bout with my disease has been real hard because this is the first time I haven't gone for the fix. I've been sharing a lot of what's going on with me in my CODA [Co-dependents Anonymous] meetings and also with my sponsor. What I've been able to do this time is grieve the loss little by little. I've wanted to hang on to the relationship (the supply) for a lot of what I still get from the memory. My supply is that I can still focus on him. I feel that by holding onto the memory that I still am loved. By my focusing still on him and feeling that he cared about me means that I don't have to feel the loss or take full responsibility for myself. So Phil's still holding onto the relationship gives me a sense of self-worth and security. Our relationship has been over for 2 years—I broke it off— this feels like such a long time to still be in a process of letting go of the relationship.

This week I ran into my other ex-boyfriend two times in the park while taking a walk. We talked both times. The first time felt right. I was able to make some amends and stay pretty clear. The second time I got into trying to let him know what's going on with me and got into trying to make him understand. I also got into wanting to be rescued. I realized how emotionally unavailable he is and that his reality is very different than mine. I still don't want to take full responsibility for my recovery from my relationship addiction with him. I found myself wanting to resolve something within the relationship as my focus and not taking responsiblity for me. I know that Bobby is an alcoholic, sex addict, and exercise addict and that we practiced our addictions together in our relationship. My sobriety is not safe around him.

After I saw him and when talking to my sponsor about my encounter with him, I was aware of my shame for having experienced being in my disease with him. She pointed out to me that being in my shame allows me to protect my supply, focus on Bobby and keeps me in my disease. I need to look at my perfection/piece of shit dualism and have had to take time to say I'm human and to forgive myself.

Today I am feeling pretty good. Lately I have been processing my grief and doing inventory on my relationships in the past and I still feel a lot of fear around being in my disease. This process is very full of feelings and breaking down my denial and letting go. I have found relief from admitting my powerlessness and still want to grab onto my wanting to take control. I have been giving myself quiet time and check-in time with others.

I think we can see several characteristic aspects of relationship addiction in this letter. Jean is afraid of being alone and knows that she is a relationship addict. She is aware that just seeing him (or thinking about him) can trigger her disease; she then becomes obsessed with him. In the past, acting on her obsession would mean getting into bed with him, which made her feel guilty and then abruptly pull away from him. She really was not looking for a sexual fix, she used sex to get her relationship fix and then felt bad about herself. However, because she is working on her recovery, she did not act on her obsession. Not acting on her obsession and getting her fix allowed her to surface her feelings and begin to do some of her grief work. It was clear from her letter that she does not even need the real person to get her fix. The memory would do. She knows that only through feeling her feelings and working through them can she hope to heal. She also knows that to do this she has to take full responsibility for herself and her life.

With the second boyfriend, Jean clearly demonstrates how getting into her disease is *her* affair and has little or nothing to do with him. Because of her relationship addiction, she was drawn to someone who had multiple addictions, and their addictions meshed well. She had found a sex addict to match with her relationship addiction. Each had her or his own disease to contend with. Jean is in recovery. Her recovery has been dependent upon her identifying her relationship addiction and working on her recovery. She could have spent years blaming these two men (and probably has); she did not really begin to recover and reclaim her power until she recognized her *disease* and worked on it.

Other Addictions Used to Justify and Rationalize

We often use our relationship addiction to justify other addictions or use other addictions to justify our relationship addiction.

Overeating, anorexia, or bulimia often go hand in hand with relationship addiction. Relationship addiction can be used to justify being attractive (i.e., very thin), or overeating can be justified by the stress and strain of relationship addiction. Chemicals are often used in conjunction with relationship addiction. Getting fat can be a way of trying to avoid the possibility of acting on relationship addiction. In psychology, we used to call this a form of reaction formation. One can be so obsessed with relationships that one does everything to avoid the *possibility* of a relationship (the relationship anorexic) and uses other addictive behavior for that purpose. It is important to remember, I believe, that even when we have a psychological concept that "explains" the behavior, it is still important to see the addictive behavior and treat it as an addiction.

The Genesis of Relationship Addiction

As I stated earlier, relationship addiction is completely integrated into the society: most of the models that we have for relationships are models of addictive relationships.

Role of the Home

It almost seems redundant to say that relationship addicts come from dysfunctional homes. Most, if not all, addicts do, and dysfunctional families seem to be the norm for the society. Why, though, do persons who come from dysfunctional families move toward one addiction and not another? Or, why when there is a learned underlying addictive process do we find certain clusters of addictions occurring in some people and not in others? I do not know. We are just beginning to learn about the differences and similarities between and among addictions, and every bit of information adds to our knowledge, understanding, and hoped for recovery.

It appears that some relationship addicts see relationships as the only way to escape a destructive, miserable home situation. The hope of a relationship is the hope of a ticket out. It is easy to see that when relationships are viewed from this perspective, persons and relationships are objectified and used as a fix. Often individuals who enter into relationships for this reason do it when young and inexperienced. They have had little or no modeling of healthy relationships at home, and they interpret the messages that they get from the culture to mean that the relationship will take care of them and give them their identity. Since such persons have few relationship skills, they look to the relationship as a magical cure. One might say they are addicted to "coupleness." Usually they have not established any identity of their own; they experience themselves as a mass of protoplasm looking for a structure, and any old structure will do. Though these characteristics are more common among Type I relationship addicts, they may be found in both types. The central, overpowering characteristic here is a complete lack of self-definition and little or no help from the family to develop it. This kind of relationship addict is an expert chameleon, adept at changing into whoever the other person wants in order to form a "relationship." They are very skilled at this. No one ever really knows who they are.

Although they have no models for relationship in their families and do not really know what relationships are, they equate relationships with survival. This is the kind of distorted thinking we see in addiction: "My parents may have a terrible relationship and they both may be sick, but at least they survived." They, then, have learned at home that to survive, however minimally, one must be in a relationship. This may be one of the things learned in families who "stay together for the children." When relationships and survival are linked in the family, this may lead to relationship addiction.

Role of the Church

The church has contributed greatly to relationship addiction. Possibly related to the church's sexual obsession, in the church, people are not considered normal unless they are coupled. Non-coupled persons are a threat in most church settings. The very setup of the social community in the church setting revolves around couples and families. Single ministers, unless they are celibate priests and nuns, are threatening to the church community, which puts tremendous pressure on young ministers (especially males) to be married before they go to their first assignment. Many seminary students I have known worked and studied so hard to get through seminary that they had no time or energy to form relationships, then were suddenly expected to marry. The church is basically a heterosexual, coupled community. To be accepted in that community, one must "fit"; there is little room for being different. There is much less emphasis on the *quality* of the relationship than there is in being *in* one.

Moreover, once a person is in a relationship, especially a marriage, he or she is supposed to *stay* in it, regardless of its quality. Even if the marriage is destructive for everyone involved, one is supposed to hold on to it. This belief has not only fostered relationship addiction, it has taught that a person has no legitimacy without a relationship. In teaching this, the church has perpetuated a concept that equates the static with security. If one can hang onto the static (what one has now) and keep it from changing, one is secure. Relationship addicts desperately seek what they believe is security, and being in a relationship, they believe, will provide it. It is ironic that individuals are willing to sacrifice their moral and spiritual values to do what they think the church wants.

Role of the Society

The norm for relationships in this society is addictive relationships, and training into relationship addiction bombards us from every direction. Earlier, I mentioned the typical "best-friend" scenario as preparation for relationship addiction. The models that children see push them into the dynamics of the best-friend syndrome. What do children learn about relationship from the society at large? They learn that there is not enough to go around. They believe that if their best friend also likes someone else, there will not be enough for them. There is never enough of anything, especially love. Since they see it all around them, they assume that jealousy is normal in a relationship, and they are constantly involved in dealing with their own feelings of jealousy.

"Best friends" learn that relationships go from one crisis to another and get "hooked" on this intensity. Jealous crisis is one form of intensity, but there are many others. What is learned is that crisis is "normal" in a relationship. To be meaningful in this society, a relationship must be intense.

Another thing learned is that partners in a relationship must *always* be together. Any time separated is meaningless and spent suffering, because the relationship is what gives meaning to existence.

During their development, children are also bombarded with popular music, which endlessly touts addictive relationships. In the lyrics they learn that they are nothing without a relationship, that relationships move from one crisis to another, that to be in relationship means to suffer, and that almost anything external to the relationship is a threat to it. Popular music reinforces the idea that one must control—hang onto—relationships or they will go away and rarely suggests that people might stay together because they want to and it is healthy to do so.

Television and movies suggest that such phenomena as instant intimacy, intensity, and dependency are the way relationships are done. One has to move fast to nail down a relationship in less than two hours!

Our entire society is organized around the heterosexual couple setting. Gays have complained about this yet have reacted by setting up the same "couple" atmosphere in gay circles. Single persons, single for whatever reason, are a threat to the "coupled society." There are very few social outlets for persons who are not part of a couple—they just don't belong. There is tremendous pressure to be in a relationship. In order to be legitimate in this society, one must be in a relationship. It is no wonder that relationship addiction is rampant. Both Type I and Type II forms of relationship addiction are not only supported, they are demanded by our society.

The Effects of Relationship Addiction on Our Society

We have learned much about relationship addiction in the last few years. One of the most important things is that it can be fatal. The stress of sick relationships can be fatal; some forms of illness appear to be related to the stress of staying in a dead or sick relationship. Many people directly trace their cancer, for example, to their relationship addiction. The very resources we look toward to help us cope with the stresses of life may well be destroying the source of life in us.

These stresses are carried into the workplace and into our major institutions. When our basic relationships are unhealthy, we ourselves are unhealthy. Relationships are important for the human organism, and they cannot give us our meaning or our identity. When we have no personal meaning or identity, we cannot possibly make our contribution to society; in this way relationship addiction contributes to society's decay.

Relationship addiction also contributes to a general feeling of dependency and a fostering of dependency in individuals. We cannot mature as a society if our members continue to function as immature, dependent children. Relationship addiction contributes to our immaturity. If we do not function as adults in our primary relationships, it is unlikely we will in the world. As I stated earlier, the United States is frequently seen as an adolescent by other nations of the world. I wonder how much our tendency to operate as adolescents is directly related to the model of relationships that is the norm for this culture.

We have seen many books on women in destructive relationships and the way that women expect and tolerate these relationships. Although there has been less writing about men hooked on relationships, I find just as many men as women relationship addicts. In men, however, this addiction is often masked by some other more blatant addiction.

Relationship addiction permeates our society and is destructive to the society as a whole. It prevents intimacy with the self or with others, and ultimately, when intimacy is not possible, war is.

The Probable Cultural Effects of Recovery

As I was preparing to write this book I was impressed that as I looked at the societal effects of recovery from each of these three addictions, I immediately came up with changes that would have to occur in the media, especially in advertising. If individuals are no longer hooked into relationship addiction, they no longer will want to listen to addictive love songs, or watch movies or television programs that portray addictive relationships. Advertising that is based upon using the right deodorant to attract a mate will not have the same meaning. The way we spend our time and money will change.

I also suspect that as more people begin to confront and recover from relationship addiction, we will find ourselves getting physically healthier. This certainly has been true in my case, and I have seen the same effect in others. I believe that we have yet to see clearly the health implications of relationships. Since we have made addictive relationships so central in this culture, they have an even greater effect on us as individuals than perhaps they should. If they were not so central, we might develop other aspects of our lives more completely.

We know, in general, that as people begin to recover from their specific addictions, they get physically healthier. What if this begins to happen on a larger scale? What will this mean for quality of life, energy, creativity, and productivity? We know that relationship addiction is killing us much younger than we would normally die. Recovery could, indeed, have some interesting implications.

Recovery could also push the church to look again at relationships and to clarify what covenant relationships might really mean without the burden of addiction. We can hardly imagine what personal freedom and intimate relationships could mean together. Yet, the combination is possible.

Unless we are willing to face up to the far-reaching implications of relationship addiction, we will never have the chance to know what relationships can be and what good relationships as the norm could mean to a society.

4. Escape from Intimacy

What do sexual addiction, romance addiction, and relationship addiction have in common? Sexual addicts "come on," romance addicts "move on," and relationship addicts "hang on." We have looked at these three addictions separately in order to understand them as separate entities. But though they are separate addictions, they do have much in common.

They do not discriminate. Anyone of any sex, race, socioeconomic status, or educational level can be affected by these addictions. Basically, addictions do not discriminate—we find them in all kinds of people—and sexual, romance, and relationship addictions can be found anywhere, any time.

All are addictions, and all three have the same characteristics as other addictions. They are progressive and fatal. They ruin individual lives, families, institutions, and whole societies. As the disease progresses, addicts become more controlling, dishonest, self-centered, perfectionistic, demanding, confused, isolated, and dysfunctional. These addictions are mind altering, like chemical addictions, and as the disease progresses, more and more of the particular "fix" is needed to get the "buzz."

In order to pursue the addiction, individuals must progressively abandon themselves. This results in ethical, moral, and spiritual deterioration, and as in other addictions, persons affected by this cluster of addictions find themselves neglecting self, children, family, work, and social responsibilities. Addicts are not able to make a consistent contribution to themselves or their society and the quality of whatever contribution they do make deteriorates.

Persons with these three addictions are in deep personal pain and become more and more powerless over their addiction and their lives.

Pseudo-relationships

All three of these addictions are primarily played out in the arena of relationships and need relationships (or, more accurately, pseudo-relationships) in order to practice their addiction. Because of this common utilization of relationships in the service of the disease, these three addictions have been confused and thought to be a single addiction.

Because they are played out in pseudo-relationships, the underlying assumption in the literature has been that these addicts are looking for loving, intimate relationships. The healthy part of the person or the nonaddicted true self may actually be looking for love and intimacy at the same time the addiction (or addictive process) is looking for its fix and utilizing relationships to get that fix. Neither the person nor the relationship is really important; they are only used to get the buzz. The pseudo-relationship addict can be just as ruthless as a drug addict in search of a fix.

Unfortunately, these addictions play upon tender, basic human needs in the service of the addiction, which makes them very confusing. Addicts almost always *require* someone else (whether it be a fantasy or a real person) to practice their disease upon, professing a need for connectedness yet treating others like objects to be used. Relationship and romance addicts use other people just as sexual addicts do. Yet all, ultimately, are avoiding intimacy and, indeed, preventing it.

We have been taught that there are certain skills and behaviors that promote and enhance the possibility of forming relationships. Unfortunately, we then experience these "skills" leading us into addictive relationships. After we see that these very skills we believe should promote intimacy are, indeed, used to avoid intimacy and practice the addiction we feel betrayed by ourselves and what we have been taught. As we list these skills, it becomes evident that they are indeed what we have been taught and what we know, and that we are at a loss to know how to form and maintain healthy relationships.

The following are some of the skills used to form pseudo- (addictive) relationships:

To be able to establish "instant intimacy."

To be able to listen even when not interested or involved in what the other person is saying.

To be able consistently to lay aside your own needs for the sake of the relationship.

To know how to "take care of" the other person and quickly move in to meet his or her needs.

To know both how to foster dependency and how to "attach" to the other in a dependent way.

To know how to "compromise" personal needs, values, ethics, or morality for the relationship (including family, children, and one's own work).

To have the ability quickly to recognize a "cosmic mate" or a "special connection."

To be able instantly to share secrets and pour out your life story.

To have an instant physical or sexual attraction.

To be able to fit the other person into romantic fantasies and/ or exotic situations having special songs, props, and symbols for the relationship even when such trappings really have little meaning except for the romantic him- or herself.

To be able to form a "connection" and not know how to be friends.

To establish an immediate intensity or "high" (being "in love") and allow that high to interfere with daily life.

To feel as though the "relationship" has you in its grip, has taken over your life, and to be able to give yourself over to that feeling.

To have the skills (imagined) and desire to "save" the other person from the life he or she has constructed.

To be willing to use the other person to escape the life you have constructed for yourself.

To define everything in one's existence in terms of the relationship and make the relationship "central" to your life.

To be able to ignore other facets of both lives for the sake of the relationship.

To have the ability to "make the other feel alive."

To be able to attract others to you, that is, to emphasize physical appearance, like dressing and fixing oneself up to attract others.

To be able to ignore aspects of the person you do not trust or like. To be able to ignore unshared values, hopes, and fears and see the other only through the eyes of illusion.

To be able to accept blame and fault for anything that goes wrong in the relationship.

To be able to "hang in there" much past the point of sanity.

To have the ability to shut off your feelings and awareness in the service of the relationship.

To have the ability to "enter into the other's world completely."

To know how to use the "skills" of communication to form immediate relationships, the "skills" being much more important than being fully present to the other person.

To be able to use manipulation and impression management to try to be what the other wants in order to "hook" the other into the relationship.

To have the ability to "take on" and "feel" others' feelings.

To have the ability to accept jealousy as an indication of true love.

To have the ability to attach yourself to people who "like" you first.

To have the ability to use "honesty" as a "con."

To have the ability to use your intuition to explain or "understand" the other.

To have developed the skills of seduction, flirtation, and titillation to a fine art.

To have the skill to look intimately involved while keeping safely hidden behind your wall.

To have learned to interpret intensity as love and, therefore, to assume that when we feel intensely about someone what we are feeling *is* love.

The ability to lose your boundaries in the relationship.
To be able to suffer endlessly for the relationship.
To be able to gaze lovingly into the other's eyes with a look re-
  sembling a dying calf in a mudhole.

We have been taught that these skills lead to relationships when,
in fact, they lead one into addictive pseudo-relationships.

Avoiding Intimacy

All three addictions appear to be seeking intimacy and all three
are escapes from intimacy. It is this aspect of these three addictions that tends to be the most confusing. The pseudo-
relationship addict uses a situation that commonly generates
intimacy to avoid it.

Most of the people who have these three addictions will loudly
protest that they are seeking an intimate relationship and that
this is what they want out of life. Unfortunately, deep within
themselves they are terrified of intimacy and run from any possibility of it.

In order to be intimate with another, one must be willing to be
intimate with oneself, and any addiction, regardless of what it is,
is an avoidance of intimacy with the self. The alcoholic clearly
moves into more and more isolation as the disease progresses in
order to protect her or his supply. That progressive isolation is
also present in the cluster of addictions we have been discussing,
but the difference is that these addicts are protesting that they
want a relationship and battering the people around them with
their confusion. It is difficult to see that a person is escaping intimacy when he or she is loudly proclaiming the need and desire
for intimacy and using a distortion of the skills that we believe
bring about intimacy. Actually, these addicts have the skills to
form pseudo-relationships; they really do not have the skills to
form genuine relationships. In an addictive society, what we
have been taught are relationship skills are really skills to form
pseudo-relationships.

For example, we have been taught in this society that in order to be "intimate" partners must be dependent upon each other. It is believed that relationships are always defined by some form of dependency whether it be dependency, independence, or interdependency. Any form of dependency is destructive. Any relationship that is defined in terms of dependency of any sort cannot be intimate. Dependency kills intimacy. Most persons believe that if one person does not *need* the other or the relationship, he or she will not stay around. That very *needing* is an invitation to the destruction of the relationship. Relationships cannot survive on dependency of any kind.

The Co-dependence, Co-addict Issue

Some definitions of co-dependence focus upon the caretaker, controller issues and assume that co-dependence is a relationship disease or, at least, one that is played out in relationships. We have also come to believe that co-dependence underlies every addiction, and some treatment centers are suggesting that recovering addicts return for treatment of their co-dependence six months to a year after treatment for their primary addiction. Needless to say, there is much confusion around the concept of co-dependence. Clearly, it has struck a chord in people, and many have self-identified as co-dependents.

For some time now, I have said that co-dependence is not just a relationship disease and that a good co-dependent does not need someone else on whom to practice his or her disease. A co-dependent can be co-dependent with a fence post.

As I have lectured about addictions and co-dependence, I have postulated the following diagram:

THE ADDICTIVE PROCESS

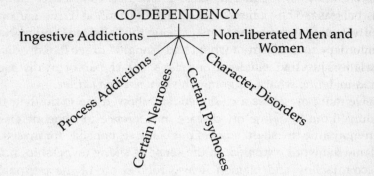

I have suggested that a basic, underlying addictive process is the norm for the society and has gone untreated. It is like the water I mentioned earlier. It can take many forms; when one avenue is blocked, it will find another. Or as Carnes says:

One of the many factors which stood out from a family perspective was that the addictive compulsivity had many forms other than alcohol and drug abuse. Also the different forms—overeating, gambling, sexuality, buying, shoplifting—all shared a similar process. And in addition, within the family, addictions would be like overlays whose reinforcing shadows simply deepened the patterns of the family pathology.

To further complicate matters, the reactions of family members to the multi-addiction patterns was as unhealthy as the coping of the addicts themselves.[1]

I believe that we have yet to treat this underlying addictive process; we must treat it *and* the specific addictions for recovery to proceed. I have further suggested that I do not know what the difference is between co-dependence and the underlying addictive process, and I believe there is one.

While doing the research for this book I have also seen many who define themselves as co-dependents who are really sex, romance, or relationship addicts (frequently relationship addicts) and who would much rather label themselves co-dependents than admit to being an addict of whatever kind. I certainly can understand this propensity, because I have found it in myself.

When I first started learning about the addictive diseases, I was sure that I was "the healthy one" and had only been affected by the disease. The "affected" not the "afflicted" as Ernie Larson puts it.[2] It took me some years of being the "affected" and working on my recovery from what I had "caught" to see that my disease was just that, *mine*—no one else's. In fact, part of my disease was to define what was going on with *me* from *outside*.

Defining myself as a co-dependent allowed me to do that. It allowed me to define my disease in reference to someone else and gave me the slight edge of not being responsible for myself. (I use the word *responsible* in the sense of taking ownership, not accountability and blame.) It also robbed me of the personal power that comes from owning myself and all aspects of myself, and it allowed me to feel slightly better than "those addicts" (which, of course, is also part of my disease). Only through my recovery work have I seen that I have the same disease (the addictive process) as everyone else in this addictive society and that it is addiction from which I must recover like everyone else—it is just that I have to recover from relationship addiction. The specific form is different from alcoholism; the underlying disease is the same. Feeling better than or not as sick as *is* my disease. Whenever I define myself in terms of someone outside myself, I am in *my* disease, and I can do that at the drop of a hat.

At some level, this is what all the "co" diseases do. Al-Anon by its very setup is defined in terms of the alcoholic, as is Adult Children of Alcoholics; Co-Sex Addicts define themselves in relation to the sex addict. In so doing we are practicing the very disease from which we are trying to recover. I know that in these groups we care encouraged to take care of ourselves and focus on ourselves, but what if we entered these groups saying "I am a relationship addict" (or a romance addict or a person addicted to suffering and pain)? We are not only powerless over what the other person does; we are powerless over our particular form of the addictive disease. Anytime we focus upon the other person in any way, we are practicing our disease, whatever form it is.

I wonder what would happen if we filtered out those aspects

of co-dependence that are sex, romance, and relationship addiction and filtered out what the underlying addictive process is. Would this take care of what we have been calling co-dependence? Are all the "co" labels a very subtle way to feel superior, to suffer, and to continue to define ourselves from outside, therefore to rob ourselves of the possibility of recovering from *our own* disease? Has this charade subtly allowed the addictive process to continue untouched, just as recovering from alcoholism but continuing to be addicted to nicotine, sugar, caffeine, work, money, or relationships allows the addictive process to continue unabated? These diseases are, indeed, cunning, baffling, powerful, and patient. Have we subtly supported the underlying addictive process with our theories? I believe we have, and I believe we have done the best we could have done. We are just learning about these diseases. We are constantly gathering more information and insight. We need to keep our understanding evolving as we continue to learn.

We first defined co-dependence in terms of the alcoholic or the addict. Beginning to see this as a disease and to see ourselves as the afflicted not just the affected (in fact, seeing that *others* were affected by *our* disease) gave us the opportunity for recovery.

What would happen if we ceased being victims and labeled our own addictions of relationship, romance, sex, work (or something yet unnamed or undiscovered) and, thereby, confronted the underlying addictive process that we all have learned in this culture?

We may find that there is, indeed, a disease we can call co-dependence. We may find, however, that we need to drop the "co" from everything and courageously face up to the reality that all these diseases are addictions and all are progressive and fatal and do not exist in a hierarchy of addictive diseases. Whenever we say that any addictive disease is more or less important or more or less serious we may, in fact, be practicing our disease.

I hope that self-defined co-dependents will read this book, reconsider, and find that they are better defined as addicts. Barbara in chapter 4 originally defined herself as a co-dependent when she started her recovery. Unfortunately, she had to hit a lower, harder bottom and almost kill herself before she realized that she was, indeed, a relationship addict in the chronic stages of her disease and that unless she faced her relationship addiction she would die.

How much of the caretaking and controlling of others that we do is in the service of our sex, romance, or relationship addiction? There may still be a place for the concept of co-dependence, and if there is, I think the concept will be much less broad than it is now. Perhaps our treatment of addictions will move to treatment of the specific forms of addiction and the underlying addictive process, or perhaps the treatment of co-dependence will become the treatment of relationship, romance, and sex addictions. We have come a long way, and I believe that we are at an interesting and exciting crossroad in our understanding of these diseases. Whatever we call them, we have discovered that these are not just psychological diseases, they are also spiritual and affect every aspect of one's being. To recover does, indeed, require an entire systems shift. The "Big Book" of Sex and Love Addicts Anonymous says it very well: "Yet, whether we were aware of it or not, an entire being had been molded by our failure, or refusal, to solve from within the problems of our real lives: insecurity, loneliness, and lack of any abiding sense of personal worth and dignity. Through sex, charm, emotional appeal, or persuasive intellect, we had used other people as "drugs" to avoid facing our own personal inadequacy. *Once we saw this, we realized that in surrendering our addictive behavior we would inevitably have to question the whole foundation of our self-image, our personal identity underlying* . . . (italics mine)." It further states: "As we came to appreciate the magnitude and mind-altering nature of sex and love addiction, and the extent to which it had perverted our value system, we had to admit that we could not reshape our whole identity unaided. . . . A need to find such a faith was the beginning of spiritual healing."[3]

Not only do we have to make a complete systems shift, we have to move into our spiritual base and recognize that all healing by definition must be spiritual. If we are truly to live out of our spiritual being we must make a systems shift from our addictive system and way of being.

Integration into Our Society

As we explore these three addictions it is easy to see that all three are integrated into our society, are supported by our society, and, indeed, themselves support the society.

In the previous chapters, we saw the role of the media, advertising, and popular music in training people into and supporting these addictions. Indeed, all three of these addictions, like alcohol, drugs, and nicotine, have their place in our economy and the worldview of our society.

The church has an especially significant role in supporting these three addictions. Sex and relationship addictions are inherent in both the general teachings of the church about relationships and its emphasis upon relationships. The sexual repression and obsession fostered by the church are fertile ground for sexual addiction, and the emphasis upon marriage in order to have approved sex is an easy precursor to relationship addiction. The church has lost much of its knowledge of covenant relationships and has often settled for the "normal" addictive relationships of the society.

Except for work and money addictions, these three addictions are probably the addictions most integrated into our society. In *When Society Becomes an Addict*, I said that the substance addictions seemed to have implications more for individuals and the process addictions broader societal implications.[4] Sexual, romance, and relationship addictions are interesting in that respect. Certainly these addictions are played out in pseudo-relationships and are destructive to individuals and families. Yet they also have broader social implications. We can only imagine the tremendous effect it would have on the economy if people actually did confront their sex, romance, and relationship addiction. For example, much of organized crime preys on these addictions as well as on addictions to drugs and alcohol. In fact, there is a great interplay between drugs and alcohol and sex and romance addiction. Large-scale recovery from these pseudo-relationship addictions could well have a dramatic effect.

These three addictions are so well integrated into our society that it is difficult to even imagine what society might be like without them. What kinds of relationships and marriages would we have without sex, romance, and relationship addiction? We can only begin to imagine. Many of us do not even know how to enter relationships that are not sex, romance, or relationship addicted. Can the church trust people to enter into committed relationships and propagate the faith and the race without buying into these three addictions? Wouldn't that be interesting to see? Is it possible that we could have healthy families because we want to be in healthy relationships and raise healthy children?

Romance and relationship addicts form what Kurt Vonnegut (in *Cat's Cradle*) calls "duprass" relationships. These are (pseudo) relationships in which the "two become one" (sound familiar?) and function and go through life as one person. These marriages often look good from the outside, but they are terrible for the children, who never feel that they can get "in" and never feel as though they belong (and they don't!). Since the marriage looks so good from the outside, the children always think there is something wrong with them and thus develop all kinds of problems. This kind of cling-clung relationship (duprass) is what our society often labels true love. We learn about these sick relationships from our society, and we do the best we can to live them out.

Intimacy and Addictive Relationships

Sexual, romance, and relationship addictions are like three strands that when combined and twisted around with one another form the braid of addictive relationships. These three addictions are the building blocks. Addictive relationships do not just spring into existence out of the blue. They have to be built.

They often are built by sexual addicts, romance addicts, relationship addicts, and people we have been calling co-dependents.

We often talk about addictive relationships as if they just *are*. But who makes them up? People do not find themselves just plopped into addictive relationships. They enter them because of their disease, their fear of intimacy, and the combined diseases of the participants perpetuate them.

We have noticed that as individuals recover from their personal addictions, their addictive relationships often collapse. (I have heard that about 80 percent collapse.) Often as people recover individually, they look at their addictive relationships and realize that there is just nothing there. They look at each other and say, "Who are you?" and they actually do not know. When two people have come together out of their disease, and they begin to recover, the pseudo-relationship they have established crumbles because, in effect, it does not really exist. They must then look to see if there is any healthy basis for a relationship beyond the disease.

Many books have been written about addictive relationships, and most of them have important information in them. What we have not clearly done is examine *how* addictive relationships result from specific addictions, especially sexual addiction, romance addiction, and relationship addiction. Also, it is important to see that addictive relationships *are*, in fact, a result of these and other addictions. So much of our writing and thinking has confused the three addictions and addictive relationships that I think it is important to look at them separately and together.

5. Addictive Relationships

The concept of addictive relationships has developed during the last few years. When this idea first emerged, to state that a relationship itself could become the addictive substance and elicit addictive behaviors was somewhat revolutionary. It was difficult to see that a person could, indeed, be addicted to a relationship or that an addictive relationship could be the result of certain addictions. What we now know is that addicts form addictive relationships.

This awareness has certainly been strengthened by the publication of such books as *Love and Addiction*, *The Cinderella Complex*, *The Peter Pan Complex*, *Women Who Love Too Much*, and *Men Who Hate Women and the Women Who Love Them*, to mention a few.[1] Clearly in this society we have begun to notice that our relationships are in trouble. They are not providing the nurturing and support that they could. They are not pathways for intimacy as we had hoped they would be, and, indeed, they probably are killing us.

I have been speaking about addictive relationships for over ten years and during that time our knowledge of the characteristics and dynamics of these relationships has progressed at a geometric rate. Let us look at some of the things we know about addictive relationships.

The Ideal Relationship

In *Women's Reality*, I discussed what I then called the Perfect Marriage.[2] An easy way to diagram that kind of marriage (which is the norm for our culture) is by using concepts from transactional analysis. There are basically three ego states within any person: parent, child, and adult. In the typical "ideal relationship," only two of these ego states are used, parent and child. The adult state goes begging.

Stability and security (both equated with being static) are the hallmarks of this kind of relationship. If either person starts to grow or change, that is seen as a threat to the relationship. For the relationship to provide security, it must remain static. If any growth does take place, it must occur within the relationship; any growth outside it is seen as a threat. In essence these "ideal" relationships are very fragile, very brittle. They cannot take much stress or change. They require an implicit contract to not be alive, and any vitality allowed must take place within the relationship. Neither person will leave the relationship because, since everything is focused on the relationship, neither believes she or he can survive outside it.

This basic ideal relationship can be diagramed as follows (the diagram applies equally to opposite-sex and same-sex relationships):

PERSON 1   PERSON 2

Parent •————————————————————• Parent
Child   •————————————————————• Child
Adult   •   • Adult

There are also the public ideal relationship and the private ideal relationship. Both must exist for this kind of relationship to be stable. In the public perfect marriage, the male (or the traditional male role) is the parent and the female (or the traditional female role) is the child. The parent-role person deals with the outside world, makes the money, makes the decisions, takes care of the car, and generally handles things outside the home. Person 2 may have no idea how to handle money, how much money the couple has, how to take care of or even drive the car, and certainly not how to deal with the world or make money. Person 2 is *dependent* upon Person 1.

In the private perfect marriage, the roles are reversed. In this relationship Person 2 is the parent, and Person 1 is the child. Person 2 runs the relationship from the inside. This person takes care of all the bodily needs of Person 1. She (or he) cooks, cleans, buys clothes, and meets sexual and social needs. Person 1 needs Person 2 to take care of him (or her) and see that daily wants and needs are cared for. Often, Person 1 does not know how to care for his or her day-to-day needs.

The relationship achieves its stability from the fact that neither person knows how to survive without the other. Some people call this interdependence. I believe that any relationship that is built on dependence of any kind is potentially destructive. Persons in this kind of relationship actually lose skills in the relationship: they give up strengths and personal power so as not to threaten "the relationship." What parades for security is really stasis and lack of vitality. The price paid for the illusion of security is high. Both must remain half-persons for the relationship to function. They contract with each other not to be "alive" or to be alive only within the relationship.

If either person starts to grow or change, he or she is perceived as betraying the contract, and bad. In this kind of relationship, the comment "You've changed" is leveled as an accusation, not an observation. One is expected to get very defensive for having grown or changed. Since growth and change are the normal state for the human organism, it is easy to see why these relationships are very brittle.

Moreover, in these relationships both parties must remember *where* they are. Behaviors that are acceptable at home are not acceptable in public, and vice versa. In *Women's Reality* I used the example of a business executive and his wife. At home, she always cut up his meat so he would not have to bother. One evening she absentmindedly reached over and started cutting up his meat when they were dining out with his superior. This wreaked havoc in the marriage. She had brought the private perfect marriage into the public arena. The fragile marriage could not tolerate this. They are now divorced. Relationships like this are indeed fragile. The "parent-child" relationship is an important aspect of the ideal relationship, an addictive relationship.

Other Characteristics of Addictive Relationships

In order to stay in an addictive relationship, people have to become progressively numb (addictions help a lot with this process!) and dishonest. They have to be dishonest about who they are, who the other person is, what they like, what they do not like, what is going on, what is not going on, and so forth. They frantically try to become what they *think* the other wants.

Partners in addictive relationships become progressively controlling, especially of themselves and what they feel. For example, they come to hate each other because of their mutual dependency and yet continue to *need* each other. One always comes to hate the person on whom one is dependent, and the person depended upon eventually begins to feel sucked dry. However, since the mutual dependency is so necessary to the relationship and is so entrenched in it, these feelings must be controlled at all costs if the relationship is to be preserved. Control of the self and of the other becomes a major focus. The dualism that one functions on in an addictive relationship is control and enmeshment at one end and abandonment at the other. One is either enmeshed and controlling or leaving. There are no other choices. Most children who have been raised with parents who were in an addictive relationship come to believe in this dualism. In fact, this is frequently what has actually happened to them. When they fight off the enmeshment and control, they are abandoned.

In this type of relationship, commitment means incarceration just as one would be committed to jail or a mental hospital. There is no concept of staying in a relationship because one *wants* to. One stays only because one is bound and cannot survive without the other person. One never sees oneself as separate but always as an extension of the other. The two are one, in the worst sense of that image.

Since so much in these relationships is built on illusion, fantasy, and dishonesty, confusion abounds. People involved in addictive relationships are always feeling confused, foggy, and slightly off base. They do not dare take time alone because to say one needs that time is terrible and is experienced by the other as an attack. Stating this kind of need is interpreted as "I want to get away from you." The assumption is that the relationship will improve if *more* time is spent together, so even when both partners need to be doing something else, they cling to each other. When this clinging becomes too oppressive, they must pick a fight so they can have time and space. People in addictive relationships never dare to become aware of their time and space needs, so their personal growth and their spiritual growth suffer greatly.

It is very difficult for anyone to take responsibility in an addictive relationship, because responsibility is always interpreted in terms of accountability and blame. Precipitating a fight is a way to get the other person to take the responsibility for leaving; one can then get the peace and quiet one needs. Frequently both want out but neither wants to be the one to leave. Addicts tend to beat up relationships. This takes the focus off of them and what they are doing or not doing with their own process. The way to avoid doing one's personal process is to pick a fight with the other person. Another variation on this theme is to focus upon what is wrong with the *relationship* all the time so there is no time to look at oneself.

In addictive relationships, both partners tend to become progressively self-centered. Neither gets his or her needs met in an addictive relationship, so there is a growing feeling that there is not "enough" and there will never be enough (which, of course, there isn't!). In response to this experience of scarcity, each person becomes more and more demanding and less willing to give to the other. This results in each getting less and less of what he or she needs and wants from the relationship, and both becoming more clutching and demanding—and the spiral continues. Often this downward spiral is aggravated by both parties looking to the addictive relationship to give them something it cannot, their own identity. Addictive relationships are supposed to "fix" both partners and take care of them. There is no concept of caring for, just taking care of. Of course no relationship can give identity to and take care of someone. Both of these processes (and they are processes) have to come from inside.

Actually, addictive relationships often function better when the parties are separated. The belief is that the relationship will be better if the two are together all the time, but since the addictive relationship is one built on fantasy, it actually works better when they are not together. It works better in fantasy than in reality. The partners are often happier with each other when they are *not* together—even on different continents. That way they can *long* for each other and not have to *deal* with each other, which is much safer.

Although both parties in addictive relationships protest loudly that they want intimacy, if intimacy walked through the room, they would both run for their lives. Addictive relationships allow each to avoid intimacy while hotly maintaining that they want it and are seeking it. This perpetuates illusion and dishonesty. Addictive relationships are actually an escape from intimacy; sexual addiction, romance addiction, and relationship addiction are safe in addictive relationships.

In order to stay in such a relationship, one has to cut off one's internal information system. Addicts are good at doing this. One has to cut off one's knowledge, one's memory, and one's information system. If these systems are alive and functioning, one cannot survive an addictive relationship. One must become a zombie.

As an addictive relationship becomes progressively intolerable, the individuals involved feel that they either have to get out of the relationship or die. Both are options that people take.

A person who decides to leave an addictive relationship feels something terrifying—a void or hole in the solar plexus. This feeling of nothingness or endless void becomes so intense when a relationship is breaking up that the person believes that he or she cannot stand it and may well die. The usual cure for this intense emptiness is to find another relationship right away.

When an addictive relationship is breaking up, it is usually very threatening to the couple's circle of friends. People who decide to recover from their addictions and leave their addictive relationships usually find the friends scurrying around attempting to maintain the status quo. These efforts may come under the guise of concern, but the strong message is "Don't shake the boat or I might have to look at myself and my relationship, and I do not want to do that, so *you stay put*." This peer pressure often makes recovery difficult; it is easy to understand why the fellowship of the twelve-step meeting is so important during recovery.

The Four Pseudo-relationships in Addictive Relationships

We see four simultaneous pseudo-relationships in addictive relationships. The first two are between masks. There is (1) my relationship with your mask and (2) your relationship with my mask. Since both people involved are defining themselves from outside, each develops a mask or an impression-managed self that she or he presents to the world. Most addicts have very low self-esteem and cannot believe that anyone would want to know or love their real self. They have to develop a mask-self that they believe will attract and please others. Both persons develop this mask-self that represents who they want to be and who they think other people want them to be; this mask is the pseudo-person that is presented for the potential relationship. Each hopes that it will please the other and holds it at arm's length to establish the relationship. This effectively sets up the charade of establishing a relationship while (supposedly) hiding safely behind the mask. One can go through the motions and not take any risks. Addicts search around for other masks that they can "relate" to without risking the terror of intimacy, and thus they form addictive relationships.

There is great fear on the part of both people that the other will peek behind the mask and see the real person. The assumption is that if you see my real person you will leave the relationship. Masks are more controlled and more controllable than real people. In an addict there is an absolute terror of knowing and being known. The masks keep the addict safe. The masks preserve the distance. The fear of seeing behind the masks or being seen behind the masks is so great that many addicts view looking behind the masks as a breach of contract by their partners and may then threaten to terminate the relationship by default. As I stated earlier, this relationship between the two masks is really two relationships, my relationship with your mask and your relationship with my mask. Neither has anything to do with who each person really is. The individuals need not and rarely do communicate much, if at all. The role of the masks is to keep people *from* knowing one another, so it is important that all communication be "mask" communication. As long as the masks stay in place, intimacy can be successfully avoided, which is necessary in an addictive relationship.

Two other pseudo-relationships that exist in addictive relationships are much weaker, yet play an important role. These two are (1) my projections on you of who I think you are and (2) your projections on me of who you think I am. These two projections or fantasy relationships have absolutely nothing to do with who each of us really is. They are mostly who the other person would *like* you to be. Addicts can be quite tenacious in holding onto their projected images and will take it quite personally if the other person acts out of character with the projected person. In fact, in addictive relationships each is busy trying to find out what the other's projected person is and become it. It is clear that there is no room for reality or anyone's real identity in an addictive relationship. The mask and the projections may be the stuff that dreams are made of, but they are not really the stuff that lives are made of.

In addictive relationships masks and projections come together to form pseudo-relationships, leaving little room for intimacy, growth, or reality. Reality is always unpopular in such relationships.

The addictive relationship is the norm in our society. We have confused true love with the cling-clung behavior of an addictive relationship. Addictive relationships always limit our lives. They do not enhance our being. Addictive relationships are often built on shame and guilt, and in an addictive society shame and guilt are seen as normal and healthy.

We have now looked at sexual addiction, romance addiction, relationship addiction, and addictive relationships. It is time to turn our attention to healthy relationships, intimacy, and recovery.

6. Intimacy and Healthy Relationships

What do we really know about intimacy in this culture? Not very much. We live in a system that is terribly threatened by it. Although we hear intimacy constantly touted, much of what we learn about it from the media and our institutions is really about a form of addiction, whether it be sex addiction, romance addiction, or relationship addiction. The relationships portrayed are usually addictive relationships. Think about the ads we see, for example. Do they teach us about intimacy? I believe they teach us more about addiction. In fact, ads often link instant intimacy with addictive agents such as alcohol and cigarettes.

In our own lives, we have few examples before us of people who really know how to be intimate and even fewer of couples who have a genuinely intimate relationship. We long for the possibility. We know that intimacy is important. We do the things we have been taught will facilitate intimacy, yet we have a strange, empty feeling that something is missing. Maybe *we* are.

Intimacy Within Ourselves

The first prerequisite for intimacy is to be intimate with oneself. As long as we are looking outside ourselves for intimacy, we will never have it and we will never to able to share it. In order to be intimate with another person, we have to know who we are, what we feel, what we think, what our values are, what is important to us, and what we want. If we do not know these things about ourselves, we can never share them with another person. Addicts cannot be intimate, because they have used their addictions to turn off their internal information systems and therefore cannot have available to themselves information about what they feel and think and who they really are.

I believe that noticing is one of the most important skills of intimacy. In order for people to know who they are, they must notice when they have to go to the bathroom. They must *notice* when they are tired. They must *notice* when they are hungry. They must notice when they like something or do not like something. They must be able to notice when they are hurt, angry, afraid, lonely, needy, happy, or at ease. So many people are unaware of themselves and so unaware of what they feel, think, and know that there is no way they could ever express themselves to someone else.

During the heyday of the human potential movement, there was a great deal of talk about expressing feelings. Many times feelings were forced, and instant intimacy was the order of the day. (Intimacy can never really be forced. It is a process, not a happening.) This movement, by encouraging people to get in touch with feelings and express them, was important historically because generally feelings had been repressed and there were many lonely powder kegs walking around. We learned much from that phase of our search for understanding of the human psyche. Some limitations from the methods of those years have now become glaringly obvious, however. First, when one feels one's feelings, one must learn what to do with them and how to express them so as not to "puke" them on everyone in sight. There was a tendency during that period (and still is with some people) to explode all over whoever was present because of feelings that were triggered by something. This frequently was not helpful either to the puker or the person puked upon. The puker often instinctively knew that the intensity of the feelings was much more than the present situation merited (in fact, it might have been buliding up for years!) and when the person puked upon retorted that the anger (hurt, fear, etc.) was inappropriate, the person doing the puking secretly knew that the other person was right and either quietly slinked off or came on even more defensive and attacking. Whatever the response, the potential intimacy of getting in touch with the feelings was destroyed. Also, puking feelings in the way I have described always created the potential for a horrendous backlash, for an even more experienced puker coming at us hot and heavy.

I believe that it is absolutely essential to get in touch with these old feelings, and the one who triggers these feelings (regardless of how obnoxious he or she seems to us at the moment) has given a really important gift to us, the gift of allowing and even assisting us to get in touch with old, buried parts of ourselves. When something is triggered for us, it is our responsibility to get ourselves to a safe place where we can work through the feelings and see what they are related to and what they mean for us. Then, we may or may not want to go back to whoever triggered us and share what part of the feelings may be related to them.

Another way that intimacy was subtly avoided (often while attesting to it) was by talking *about* feelings and not feeling them as they were discussed. Some people are very expert at talking *about* feelings; they are just not very good at *doing* them. They are not good at being congruent within themselves about what is going on inside and what is being expressed outside. To be intimate with ourselves we must have this kind of congruence.

I had a friend who once said that he believed that a relationship was simply being present to another person. I believe intimacy with oneself is simply being present to oneself and then being able to bring that self into relationship with others. In order to be intimate with another person, one must be intimate with oneself.

Once there is a certain modicum of knowledge, information, awareness, and presence with the self, there is a possibility of sharing that process that is the self with another. This, then, is the potential of intimacy between two people. If, however, one is not living one's own process, it is never possible to share that process with another person or other people.

Intimacy with Others

Now, what about intimacy in relationships? Let us first look at four key behaviors that interfere with intimacy. They are first, not taking responsibility; second, maintaining the illusion of control;

third, being dishonest; and fourth, being self-centered. Doing any one of these four is guaranteed to destroy intimacy and destroy relationships. Addictive relationships are built on these processes.

Let me start with self-centeredness. When we are self-centered, it is difficult for us to see our partner as separate from ourselves and/or the relationship. Self-centered people tend to interpret their partner's feelings or acts as being either for or against themselves, and they react accordingly. This effectively puts them at the center of the universe seeing everything as defined in relation to them. For example, if our partner loves someone else, that is against us and means that we are not loved; there surely could not be enough love to go around. Another way of being self-centered in a relationship is to assume that whatever the partner feels or thinks has been caused by me. Therefore, when the partner is "down" or depressed, the question is always, "What have I done?" What looks like concern is actually self-centeredness. The assumption is that if something is going on with the other person, I must have caused it. There is no place for self-centeredness in healthy relationships. In order to live in process in relationships, we have to see the other person as separate *and* equal, paradoxically knowing that we all are one. Is it any wonder that we mistakenly think that addictive relationships are easier? The known, even when it is not working at all or is destroying our soul, often feels safer and easier than the unknown.

Dishonesty is something that is well known in our society. We have become so inured to dishonesty, our own and others', that it takes effort to recognize the subtleties of the "the con" in ourselves and other people. Relationships are so important to us and we feel so alienated and isolated without them (especially when we do not have ourselves) that we often "slip" in our quest for truth for what we think is "in the service of our relationship." Dishonesty never benefits a relationship, regardless of the reason we give ourselves. Usually when we say that we do not want to hurt someone, what we really mean is that we do not want to face and have to deal with his or her reaction to the truth. Always, the first person we lie to is ourselves, and lying to ourselves is just as destructive to the relationship that we have or need to have with ourselves as it is to our relationships with others.

The basic dishonesty that we practice in relationships is often that of not being honest about and true to our own process and of not doing it. We "sacrifice" for the relationship, which often means not doing the things we want or need to do even when they would have no effect on the relationship. For example, I recently visited an old friend in the East. In the course of our discussion, she mentioned that she would like to have a cottage on the beach as she loves the ocean and would like to retreat there to write and think. She can easily afford it, so I said, "I think you should do that." She then replied (with much bitterness and anger in her voice) that she could not do that because her husband does not like the ocean. She followed that with, "One has to make sacrifices for a marriage." Her bitterness pushes her to be controlling and angry. She needs to be honest with herself and work through these feelings about control—about giving and not giving, about marriage meaning that the partners are Siamese twins, about doing things separately, about sitting on the truth as a control mechanism and so forth—to give their marriage the possibility of being alive. Let us look at some of the factors involved here.

She is a writer. When she is working on a project, she withdraws almost completely and focuses upon her work. Many writers have to do that. Her husband has his own life and does not seem to suffer greatly when she is absorbed in a project. If she does her writing at a beach cottage (not far away) and comes home on weekends or he visits for weekends, they might have as much or more quality time together as they normally do. In fact, there might be less stress on both of them if they did something like this when she is working on something (she does tend to have a laserlike focus when she is working). She could be in a setting that is conducive to her writing and might be even more efficient and productive.

She may be into her relationship addiction, wanting something from her husband that is not possible or appropriate for a relationship and caught in the typical relationship addiction illusion that if they spend *more* time together, she will get what she wants. She may not trust the relationship or her husband and be afraid not to be around (to control him?).

She may be afraid to have a cottage and to be there alone, or she may not even really want the cottage yet want to make him responsible for her not having it. She may be into an image of being a martyr and attaching this need to a beach cottage. She may be afraid to be with herself and her writing and creativity (I can understand that one!) and want her husband to take the responsibility for that. Her husband may be a complete monster and pitch a fit no matter what she wants to do. There are many possibilities.

Whatever the situation, she needs to be honest with herself and work through her feelings so she can share those feelings and how they relate to her partner. The "cottage issue" offers a wonderful possibility for intimacy through honesty if they can only embrace it. Perhaps it is just this possibility that is so frightening to both of them. She is not being honest unless she works through her feelings and shares them. To be in process relationships, we have to take the responsibility for owning our feelings and for doing our process as honestly as we can so we do not puke our feelings and our process on our partners. This means that we have to work with what is going on with us, take responsibility for that, and then honestly communicate whatever it is. If we have partners who handle our sharing roughly or violently, we need to take a serious look at why we chose this kind of person for a partner.

I think honesty is also related to not puking our process on our partners. From my experience, most fights and most tension between partners are related to puking one's process on the other. This is a form of dishonesty. When I am not taking responsibility for my own process I am being grossly dishonest. (For example, my friend may have been terrified of facing her creativity and work, needed to do it, but chose to blame her husband for her not doing it.) In this kind of dishonesty I am not seeing what is going on with me and sharing that as best I can. In fact, my own observation is that people who tend to operate in an addictive way tend both to avoid working with their own processes and to puke them on others. That is one of the ways one can use the relationship as a fix. When I want to avoid my own process (which frightens me, especially because I do not know where it will lead me), I pick a fight with my partner (puke); the fight can then become the focus and get me off the hook of dealing with myself. Indeed, the fight distracts both of us from having to take responsibility for our own process. If we have a good addictive partner (self-centered), he or she will always be willing to play the game. Because of their own self-centeredness, addictive partners do not want to be left out of the action; thus both are absolved of dealing with being stuck in their own process. When I hear a statement like "One has to sacrifice for a relationship," I see it as a red flag indicating an addictive relationship.

Also, frequently our reaction to something our spouse is saying or doing has nothing to do with our spouse at all. Something may be arousing old feelings of abandonment, feelings about the loss of the illusion of control, fear of the loss of love, or any other unresolved feeling. When we follow our process and learn from where it leads us, we can see that whatever our partner has triggered is a gift, an opportunity to learn from our process.

This does not mean that we have to put up with whatever our partners do. As we do our own process and become more clear about it, we can give our partners more honest information about our needs and wishes. We may have chosen partners who are not able to handle our honesty at that time—or ever. At least if we are honest and take responsibility for ourselves, we have the information reality provides us, and we can make our decisions based upon it. This knowledge may mean that we have to let go of our illusion of the relationship and decide to stay in it with full knowledge of present limitations (which may change as we change). On the other hand, our awareness may result in our realizing that we have to let go and cannot tolerate or do not wish to live with the other person's process. Whatever our decision, we have made it out of honesty and clarity.

As we respect our process and our partner's process, we have to do all kinds of letting go. As I have said before, if we choose to live in process, we cannot let *anything* (our work, relationships, money, sex, etc.) interfere with our process (our sobriety, our spirituality). All the recovery programs say that in order to recover, we have to be willing to put our sobriety first. If we do, we may not have to give up anything. We do, however, have to be *willing, open, and ready* to give up anything if it distracts or threatens our sobriety. In its early stages, more things threaten our sobriety. Therefore, until our sobriety is well established, we may have to walk a narrower path. When we live our relationships with a similar awareness, they become much more peaceful and enjoyable.

Now is the time for a word about expectations and control in relationships. Whenever we get into expectations, we are moving into our illusion of control. We need to be clear on what we want and then be willing to let it go. When we try to make things come out the way we want them to, we are slipping into a control system (addiction). Frequently, much of our reality is based upon subtle control. We believe if we act a certain way we can make our partner love us and want to stay in the relationship. Love does not work like that. It cannot be controlled. It is a gift. We must respect that even if someone has promised to love us forever (a concept that comes from the addictive system). They or we cannot make such a promise if we live in process. We may love one another forever *and* our processes may take us in different directions. However, if our thinking does not come out of a scarcity model or a dualistic model, it may turn out that even if our processes do take us in different directions, our relationship may not be destroyed and it *and* the new direction may be true and right. It is only when we try to control ourselves *and* the other that we get into trouble.

This does not mean that when we live in process relationships we cannot have feelings. Not only do we have feelings, we may have more because we are not living behind the mask of addictions and are in touch with our feelings. We will have the whole range of feelings: joy, pain, anger, hurt, confusion, excitement, vitality, sadness. Having feelings is part of being human, and we are talking about human relationships here, not relationships between deities (which we sometimes attempt!). Fortunately, we do not die from having feelings. In fact, it may well be that we die from *not* feeling our feelings and working them through. Each feeling is an opportunity for growth if we can but take it.

As we try to live in process and not puke our process on those we love, we open the door to new ways of relating and being with one another. Many of us have confused love and control. We assumed that if we do not try to control our partners, we do not love them *and* if they do not try to control us, they do not love us. What a waste!

Many have talked about the key role that dependency plays in addictive relationships. Certainly, to begin to recover one must face the extreme dependency that means addiction. Addiction is dependency. The very fact of addiction assumes dependency. Yet the forms dependency can take in addictive relationships are fascinating.

We have long wondered why persons in destructive, battering relationships do not just get out. The more we understand the powerlessness of addiction (sex, romance, and relationship) and addictions as an addictive disease that is progressive and fatal, the more we understand the stranglehold of dependency and addiction. Addictive relating erodes the psyche and the being so much that often those in addictive relationships are too battered and bewildered to quit or get out. In a really sick addictive system (such as some marriages) the individuals lose touch with reality to such a degree that they have no basis for judgment. They are being smothered by the disease. These people are victims of addictive relationships and an addictive culture, and they are victims of their own disease. Before they can change the relationship or the culture, they need to do their own healing and recovery. This is the only way to personal freedom.

There has been a great hue and cry from some people in the movement around battered women that those of us who are encouraging women to claim their own addiction in relationships are not feminists. These critics are telling us that we are telling women that they are sick (bad!) and are not properly seeing that women are victims of the system and need to fight the system.

First, to say someone is dependent and has the disease of relationship addiction (sex, romance, or some other addiction) is not to say that person is bad. It is, in fact, to recognize that women have been severely affected by this addictive culture—as we all have. To say we are all addicts is to give all of us the possibility of recovery from a disease inherent in our addictive culture. Only by owning our addictions can we recover from them. Moreover, victims never recover. They just stay victims—victims of men or victims of women. Victims need the safety to feel and work through their feelings of hurt, anger, rage, fear, and loneliness. If they are encouraged to work those feelings out on the addictive society, they not only feed that sick society, they are being set up for harsh and bitter backlash. We know that we can buy into a sick society in two major ways. One is to go along with it; the other is to adopt its methods and use those methods to fight it. When we do the latter, we have become just like the society and are, indeed, feeding its sickness.

To wrench free from destructive relationships, we must see that we have been victims—have been battered—we must do our process work around this, work through our feelings, and move on. When we puke our process on others, we always get backlash, and down deep somewhere inside ourselves, we know that the feedback we hear that our behavior is inappropriate rings true; instead of regaining our self-respect, we feel worse about ourselves.

We must recognize that to recover from the sickness of an addictive society that has imprisoned us in our addictions we must go through our own levels of truth toward our own healing. First we must admit and see that there is a problem; then we must have the time and safety to work through our feelings; then we must own our part in buying into a sick system. If we do not take the step of owning our own complicity in this system, we run the risk of selecting new oppressors—even women who have not adequately dealt with their own rage and are asking women who have been battered in relationships to go out and be battered by the system with the backlash that comes from attack.

To recover, we must take responsibility (not accountability and blame but ownership) for our personal addictive process and our complicity with the system that is destroying us. It is as we respect each individual's processing through victim, that we no longer are victims.

I have noticed some rather interesting aspects of dependency that seem to be present in addictive relationships. One aspect that is really an outgrowth of defining oneself from the outside is particularly interesting.

I have a friend who absolutely refused to terminate a destructive relationship. Initially, he appeared quite dependent (which he was), and it appeared that it was his dependence that kept him in the relationship (it was not). My friend was a romance addict and impression management was his most important concern. He *looked* dependent, and his main concern was really that he not be seen as the one who did not hang in with the relationship or the one who terminated it. He simply would not risk being seen as a bad guy.

The addict frequently sees responsibility as accountability and blame, and the relationship, sex, or romance addict (co-dependent) *does not want to be blamed*. In recovery, we know that to take responsibility means to *own* one's life. Yet, the person not in recovery cannot make this distinction and sees taking responsibility as being blamed. Because addicts and what we have called co-dependents have such low self-esteem, they do not feel that they can tolerate being "blamed" and held accountable for the demise of the relationship, especially if that is something they secretly wish for. Being unable to accept this responsibility also contributes to the continuation of the denial system, which, of course, perpetuates the disease and keeps one in the destructive relationship.

I certainly know about this process personally. I can remember when I had not really started my recovery and I needed to get out of a destructive marriage. I kept telling myself and others that my husband and I just could not make it and the marriage was a failure. I deluded myself into believing that if we could just go to counseling and make the marriage work, I would be more than happy to stay in it. Then, one day, I had to get honest and face myself and my own self-deception and realize that even if we could make the marriage better, I did not want to live with that man. I had left the marriage, psychologically, some years back when, at crucial times for me, he simply could not be there—or so it seemed. However, I did not want responsibility for the demise of the marriage, so I continued the charade. Now, in my sobriety, I could no longer do that.

In admitting that I was not willing to stay in the marriage even if it could be improved, I broke through my denial system, and I was able to be honest with myself and others and take responsibility for terminating the marriage. The process of taking responsibility for my own wishes and decisions strengthened my recovery and contributed to my healing. There is freedom in taking responsibility for one's own life and wishes even when it does not fit with culturally approved behavior. Often addicts (and codependents) do not feel strong enough to take responsibility for their lives. Yet when they do, paradoxically, they become stronger.

A friend of mine pointed out that often individuals who fit into the constellation of pseudo-relationship addictions need an extraordinary reason for leaving a relationship or situation. They cannot just leave because it is the right thing for them to do or because they need to. It has to be a big deal. They may have to discredit the other person in order to feel justified in leaving. Since most addicts feel so unworthy, leaving for their own good is not a good enough reason.

Another "leaving technique" we often find is that of provoking the other person until he or she kicks them out. They then can be blameless, righteous, *and* pathetic and can feel justified in seeking sympathy and support. Addicts cannot imagine seeking support when it is they who terminate the relationship; therefore, they assume that if they take that step they will be abandoned, isolated and alone. There is nothing more bloody than two of these addicts trying to leave the relationship and beating each other up emotionally and physically to get the other to take the responsibility to leave. The sad thing is that if each could take responsibility for her or his process and both say what they want and need, they might not have to leave at all.

Much of this behavior is motivated by fear. Fear is different from dependency, yet they often go hand in hand. Dependency is probably a result of fear. I have found that most people who stay in destructive relationships are afraid of their mates and afraid of leaving. They become progressively fearful. As I talk with them, it is clear that they have lost touch with their reality and sometimes cannot even articulate what they fear or what they suspect their spouse might do. (Of course, in violent, battering relationships, they *know* what their spouse might do.) When one is afraid, it is impossible to act, and maintaining the status quo feeds the illusion of control.

It is easy to see why intimacy is so impossible in these kinds of relationships. One is kept so busy with the addiction that intimacy is smothered (even if it could grow in this soil, which it can't). I believe what Jed Diamond[1] calls approach-avoidance is actually carefully programmed avoidance of intimacy. To be intimate is to be present—with oneself and others—and this is impossible in addiction.

No discussion of intimacy would be complete without a mention of physical intimacy and sexual intimacy. These arenas have become very confused in our addictive society. Not all intimacy is physical, and not all physical intimacy is sexual. Both are important; neither happens in pseudo-relationships. Physical and sexual conning are used to get the "fix" and usually have nothing to do with intimacy or loving. This is confusing to both partners, because the very approaches that one would expect to facilitate intimacy usually destroy it.

Genuine sexual and physical intimacy usually grow out of a process of intimacy that has some history. Whenever the first step to relationships is physical or sexual or is a physical or sexual attraction, red warning lights for addiction should be flashing.

True intimacy is a process that grows over time. It is a process of knowing and being known, and it requires openness and willingness from each person involved. Intimacy has no techniques. In spite of the how-to books that tell us all we have to do is follow the manual, intimacy cannot be orchestrated. It starts with the self, knowing the self and being present to the self.

In *Women's Reality*, I discussed the concept of love in what I then called the Emerging Female System (now the Living Process System).[2] I described love as an infinity sign that goes between two people. It is an energy exchange that leaves the heart area of one person and enters the solar plexus of the other. It then moves up the body, that person takes some because she/he is loved and adds even more because one is loving. It then moves to the heart area (heart chakra) and is sent back to the other, and the whole process is repeated.

The entire process is very fragile and can be blocked at any step along the way. If a person feels angry or stingy, she or he does not send it. If the person to whom it is coming feels blocked or angry, it does not get in, or if that person feels unworthy or unlovable he or she will not take some out . . . and so it goes. When the whole process is complete there is an infinity sign of love moving between two people—or even among many.

However, for this infinity sign to function there must be two prior infinity signs operating. Each person must have intimacy with his or her own self for the interpersonal infinity sign (or intimacy) to happen. It can be drawn thus:

PERSON 1   PERSON 2

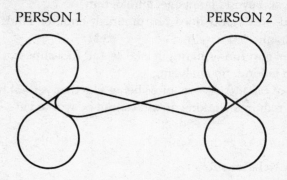

Strange, isn't it? This is what intimacy looks like when diagrammed.

The prerequisites for intimacy are

- Loving someone (being a lover)
- While staying with yourself and
- Fully participating in your own life

Intimacy is not static. It is always moving to a new level. It is an energy flow with no barriers. Intimacy cannot be controlled. Like a feeling, it cannot be held onto or reproduced at will. We notice intimacy. We do not produce it. Intimacy is

Knowing and being known by another
Sharing information openly
Stroking
Not necessarily romantic or sexual
Being alive and sharing that sense of aliveness
Being intimate with the self first
Experiencing life together—developing a common history
Involves all the senses
Not brought about by techniques
Not confined to time and space—one can remain intimate

without contact, allowing the other to go away when she or
he needs to

Magical, beyond language, a hologram

Varied—one kind does not diminish another kind; there is
enough

Playful and fun—sharing mistakes and foolishness

Much talking, no analyzing

A lot of paradoxes—requires being together yet not having to
be; requires working at, yet cannot be worked at

A gift

Healthy Relationships

In chapter 5 we looked at the simultaneous relationships that
are occurring in addictive relationships. There are four, two mask
relationships and two projected relationships. Neither has anything to do with the other person or with reality.

In healthy relationships, there are five simultaneous relationships happening. Healthy relationships are based upon each
person having a relationship with him- or herself. The relationship with the *self* is the basic building block of relationship. Both
parties must have broken through their denial systems to some
extent, achieved some modicum of honesty with themselves,
and become willing to take responsibility for themselves. In general, each must be a person in his or her own right. If one does
not have a relationship with the self, it is truly impossible to have
a living process (healthy) relationship; it will not be possible to
be honest with the "other" if one is not in contact with oneself.

This relationship with the self is a source of pleasure and ex-
pansion and needs time and nurturing in order to grow. In order
to have a relationship with the self, it is necessary to have quiet
time alone, time to enrich one's spirituality. A relationship with
the self takes time. I believe this relationship with the self includes a relationship with God, or a Higher Power, however one
conceptualizes that. Truly having a relationship with our own
process relates us to the process of the universe.

The next two relationships that occur in healthy relationships are each person's fantasied relationship with the other. Each person has a fantasy about what is going on with the other and about who the other is. In addictive relationships, this is enough and is similar to, but different from, the projected relationships. In healthy relationships, it is necessary to bring these fantasied relationships into the conscious self, explore them, and make them available to and share them with the other. Only in doing so can we provide ourselves with reality checks. These relationships can be the source of a lot of fun, and as long as we know them for what they are, can add richness to our relationship with ourselves and with others. In addictive relationships these fantasied relationships run wild, are not subject to reality checks, and can be destructive to the self and the relationship.

A fifth relationship in healthy relationships is the acutal relationship that exists between the two people. This is what we previously called the infinity sign going between two or more people. It is dependent upon the previous four having been developed, maintained, and "cleaned up" if necessary. Not that we have to be perfect to have a relationship; relationships provide a major arena for growth and self-awareness, and paradoxically they have to exist consciously and be worked with for the relationship between the self and the other to develop. This relationship between the self and other(s) requires taking risks (not that the other four relationships do not!). In order to have this relationship, it is necessary to be able to see the self and the other and to respect the process of both. This relationship is a rich source of information for the self. And it is more than that; it is an opportunity to know and be known.

Addictive relationships are missing this fifth relationship. People in addictive relationships are always talking about working on "the" relationship when, in truth, it does not exist. I find in healthy relationships one almost never has to work on *the relationship*. If the other four are happening, this one is quite easy.

In healthy relationships, the focus is upon respecting one's own process. When this happens, each—almost by default—respects the other's journey and supports it as well as his or her own.

Healthy relationships imply supporting each other, yet there is no focus upon "fixing" the other person. Each person's process is respected and it is recognized that each must do what he or she must. It is understood that if I have feelings about what the other does, these are *my* feelings and I have to handle them as best I can. Commitment is not incarceration. It is each being committed to her or his own process, sharing that process, and respecting the process of the other. This includes respecting the other's need for personal time for spirituality.

A healthy relationship is an open system, which means that both information that is internal to the parties and the relationship and information that is external to the parties and the relationship are sought, listened to, and resolved. Both recognize that this relationship is not isolated and "special" (i.e., "terminally unique"), that it exists in a greater context while itself being very important. Therefore, in healthy relationships, choices are very important, and the generation of options opens the possibility to growth and creativity. Choices are not threats.

In chapter 4 we listed some of the common "skills" used to form addictive relationships. What would a counterlist look like for healthy relationships? Of course, we know that we cannot manipulate intimacy or healthy relationships, yet because so little is truly known in this area, it is fun to play around with some ideas.

To be able to to "wait with" the evolution of a relationship.
To be able to be honest when one is not interested or cannot listen.
To recognize and accept one's own needs and honor them.
To care for, not take care of, the other.
To know that dependency in any form kills relationships; to honor the integrity of the self and the other.
To know that one cannot compromise one's spiritual and moral values without eroding the relationship.

To be present to the self and the other and share intimacy where appropriate.

To know that physical loving evolves as intimacy grows.

To know the relationship is only one important aspect of one's total life.

To be unwilling to turn one's life over to anyone.

To accept responsibility for one's own life and recognize the other's responsibility for his or her own life.

To be honest with oneself about who the other is and what important values, hopes, and fears are not shared.

To see the other and the self clearly, without judgment.

To know that blame has no place in intimacy and to be willing to own one's mistakes without judgment.

To be unwilling to accept physical, emotional, or spiritual battering.

To be able to share "worlds" while maintaining one's own.

To be present.

To take risks and be vulnerable with the other.

To share feelings as one feels them.

To have and respect boundaries.

To know that suffering is not love—pain will occur; suffering is a choice.

To live one's own process and respect the process of the other, whatever it is.

To give information and to let it go without trying to control what the other does with it.

To know that love cannot be created or manipulated. Love is a gift.

All of us are pioneers exploring the potential in relationships. We are learning together. In healthy relationships, we are always flying by the seat of our pants. When we are not trying to control, not trying to create an atmosphere of stasis or security, we are always evolving with the relationship.

In this kind of relationship, there is always an awareness of being a part of a holographic, evolving universe in which we have a part to play. When we are in our addictive process we come to believe that we cannot stand these evolutions and changes. We can and we must if we and our relationships are to be alive.

We have everything we need to live in process. We have everything we need to live in a process way. Yet as Diane Fassel says, there is *no transformation without recovery*.[3] We cannot just find a new therapy or a new spiritual path. Moreover, there is no recovery without transformation. The two processes must happen simultaneously and support one another. There is no external answer. We must face the ways that we have bought into and practiced the addictive process in order to move on to being healthy and forming healthy relationships.

7. Recovery

When we speak of recovery, we must remember several things about the pseudo-relationship addictions we have been discussing, a constellation of addictions that interact to reinforce the addictive process and result in addictive relationships.

- *It is important to see these syndromes and patterns as addiction.* The usual psychiatric and psychological techniques have not been very effective with these behaviors. Yet when we treat them as addictions and work with them as addictions, improvement occurs. As Carnes says, "Nor has there been, heretofore, an integrating concept—such as addiction—which makes connections within patterns of behavior for researchers to use."[1] This "integrating concept" may well help us understand behaviors and situations that previously may have been misunderstood and that have basically gone untreated.
- *It is important to see that we are dealing with three, maybe four, forms of addiction,* all of which emanate from a basic underlying addictive process. Sex addiction, romance addiction, and relationship addiction are all forms of addiction that have similarities and differences and also overlap. What we have called co-dependence may exist in its own right in addition to these other three, and if it does, it is a form of addiction. It is not "caught" by contagion, nor is it a lesser form of addiction than the others.
- *In order for recovery to proceed, we must treat the separate addictions and the underlying addictive process.* Treating one *or* the other will not suffice. We must see how these addictions are separate and how they interact.
- *All these addictions are escapes from intimacy.* It may *appear* that

they seek intimacy, but in reality these addictions actually *avoid* intimacy. The inner person, the sober person, may want intimacy, but none of these addictive processes can achieve intimacy.

- *All these addictions are life-threatening.* As the basic text for the Augustine Fellowship states: "Perhaps progression was the key, driving at the fact that once we had lost control over how often or how long we engaged in sexual and emotional indulgences, there was no way that we would avoid, over the long run, a critical threat to sanity, and even to life itself. Our condition was, indeed, one of powerlessness and hopelessness."[2] These addictions are fatal. As Kasl says of sexual addiction, "It is serious. It is serious. It is serious."[3]

- *All these addictions are integrated into the culture and supported by the culture.* There are cultural and financial reasons for these addictions; persons needing to recover cannot expect much support from the system. This point leads to the following point.

- *In order to recover from these addictions, one must have ongoing support.* This is one of the reasons that the Twelve-Step Program is so important. According to one of its sayings, "Recovery is something one has to do *oneself*; one does *not* have to do it *alone*."

- *These addictions are extremely difficult and painful to confront because they use the very skills we have learned for approaching intimacy and relationships to avoid intimacy and relationships.* As Carnes says, "What makes the sexual addict different is that he [sic] draws upon the human emotions generated by courtship and passion."[4] This can also be said for romance and relationship addicts. The skills may be the same. The way they are used is quite different. Yet I now wonder if the skills that we *believe* lead to relationships actually lead only to addictive relationships. We have a whole new set of skills to learn if we are to have healthy relationships.

- *These addictions are often related to early sexual abuse by individ-*

uals and institutions. Because of early abuse, sex, romance, and relationships are often confused in the minds and beings of children as they grow up. Frequently addictive behaviors in relationships are all that one has learned and then, consequently, later practiced.

- *Often those protesting the most about wanting intimacy are those who do not know how to be intimate and are using pseudo-intimacy and pseudo-relationship as a fix.* I am suspicious of those who attend twelve-step meetings (or anywhere else) and announce that they are "ready for a relationship." Frequently, they are looking for a fix, not sobriety.

- *Maybe one of the reasons that treatment for drug and alcohol addiction is so difficult and relapse so frequent is that the treatment programs do not treat the constellation of addictions.* We know that recovery is hard and that sobriety is fragile. Everything around us invites us back into our disease. It is only when we accept and work with the broader picture that we can effectively work with addictions.

- *Recovery is a process, not a happening.* Recovery does not happen all at once, nor is it linear. Addiction is more "normal" for our society. The disease is always there "lurking" to invite us back in. Fortunately our healthy being—our sober self, our process spirituality—is always there also. We have but to do our footwork. I have sometimes been criticized because I do not have how-to exercises in my books. But there is no easy way, and the often-offered "fixes" may themselves actually perpetuate our addictions. Recovery is a long, difficult, and exciting process and one that a person has to work at.

- *Recovery is possible.* We can, indeed, be sober and fully alive. It may not always be easy and it may not always be fun, and it is always interesting. We often dwell on how difficult recovery is, yet in my experience and in what I know of others' it is a lot easier and better than living addictively.

- *Recovery is a miracle.* When we think about the grip our addictions had on us, how well we were trained into them, and how prevalent they are all around us, how much the norm for the society, it is truly a miracle that anyone recovers; yet millions do.

- *Our living process (our sobriety, our spirituality) is also cunning, baffling, patient, and powerful, or recovery would not be possible.* Sometimes we just give the disease too much power. When we think how we have pushed down our process, ignored it, and avoided it with any number of addictions, it is a wonder it is still there. Yet *it is*! I find this truly a latter-day miracle.
- *The Twelve-Step Program is the most effective way to recovery.* Like Melody Beattie (who says it much better than I) can strongly say, "I unabashedly love Twelve-Step Programs." They are

not merely self-help groups that help people with compulsive disorders stop doing whatever it is they feel compelled to do (drinking, helping the drinker, etc.). The programs teach people how to live—peacefully, happily, successfully. They bring peace. They promote healing. They give life to their members—frequently a richer, healthier life than those people knew before they developed whatever problem they developed. The Twelve-Steps are a way of life."[5]

Resistance

Before I actually *tried* the Twelve-Step Program, I had many criticisms of it. Although I thought these criticisms were quite unique and creative, they are the ones I often hear from others, so perhaps they were not as good as I thought. I will share some just for fun.

- Aren't the Twelve Steps just another form of substitute addiction? People seem to have to go to meetings all the time and to use them as an addiction.

    Certainly people in early recovery go to a lot of meetings, and they may even use the twelve steps addictively. That is not the program; that is the addict. Fortunately, in spite of the addict the program works.

- The Twelve-Step Program seems rigid and controlling. Aren't the steps just another fix?

  Again, they *can* be used that way, and fortunately (*unfor*-tunately for the addiction), they work.

- I have seen people go to twelve-step meetings and not get any better. How do you explain that?

  I have seen people go to therapy, to hospitals, and to all kinds of places and not get better. "Getting better" is up to the individual. The program is not magic. It is a way. "We have to do it ourselves. We do not have to do it alone."

  Also, although some people get somewhat better by attending meetings, real sobriety is a process. There is a great deal of difference between attending meetings and *working* a program. I have never seen someone actually *working* a program who did not get more sober.

- I have nothing in common with those people; why should I attend twelve-step meetings?

  Yes you do. To me that sounds like the disease talking. It is called terminal uniqueness.

- The meetings do not seem that clear to me. How can I recover there?

  Of course they seem unclear at times, they are a meeting of addicts, for heaven's sake! The idea is to get out of *any* meeting what is there for you and leave the rest. What one takes home is often more of an indication of one's willingness and openness than it is of what is or is not happening at the meeting. Judgmentalism is a characteristic of the disease.

- People who attend twelve-step meetings leave their family and their old friends and make the program and program people the center of their life. There must be something wrong with that.

  This is often true. Early in recovery, one needs the support of other recovering people and the wisdom and modeling of those who have a good sobriety and long years of recovery. After one's recovery is better established, it is really a drag to be around people who choose to stay in their addictive process.

Recovering people are willing to do twelve-step work and support those who show some openness and willingness; they are not willing to waste their time with those choosing to stay stuck. This choice is made not out of disease; it is made out of health and recovery.

This is only a sample of criticisms. I find that they are usually made by persons who have not really tried the program or really worked the steps. There is a great deal of difference between going to meetings and actually working the steps. The steps have to be worked every day and repeated endlessly. The level on which one is working them changes, and the perspective changes constantly as recovery proceeds.

All this is not to try to sell the program. I would never do that. This is a program of attraction, not promotion. However, I thought it might be helpful to share some of the judgments I made before I began *working* the program and that I have since heard. I continue to grow in my respect for the trickiness of this disease and the effectiveness of the program.

I do not want to go into much detail about the specific steps. Many have done that; their treatments of the steps differ and all are extremely helpful.

I have nothing but respect for the text for the Augustine Fellowship called *Sex and Love Addicts Anonymous;*[6] next to the "Big Book" of Alcoholics Anonymous,[7] it is the best book I have seen for clarifying the experiences of one in the disease and doing recovery. Both of these are books to go back to again and again. It will be necessary to substitute romance and relationship addiction (and delete "love," I believe) in these books. That is not so difficult.

Also, Carnes does a good treatment of the Twelve-Step Program from the perspective of his scheme in *Out of the Shadows.* I recommend reading his discussion.

Also helpful is Melody Beattie's discussion of the Twelve-Step

Program from the perspective of co-dependence. Making the connection between co-dependence and the addictions discussed in this book is easy, and her treatment of the Twelve-Step Program is excellent.

Working the Twelve Steps

The following are the Twelve Steps from Alcoholics Anonymous and Sex and Love Addicts Anonymous.

THE TWELVE STEPS OF
ALCOHOLICS ANONYMOUS

1. We admitted we were powerless over alcohol—that our lives had become unmanageable.
2. Came to believe that a Power greater than ourselves could restore us to sanity.
3. Made a decision to turn our will and our lives over to the care of God *as we understood Him*.
4. Made a searching and fearless moral inventory of ourselves.
5. Admitted to God, to ourselves, and to another human being the exact nature of our wrongs.
6. Were entirely ready to have God remove all these defects of character.
7. Humbly asked Him to remove our shortcomings.
8. Made a list of all persons we had harmed, and became willing to make amends to them all.
9. Made direct amends to such people wherever possible, except when to do so would injure them or others.
10. Continued to take personal inventory and when we were wrong promptly admitted it.
11. Sought through prayer and meditation to improve our conscious contact with God *as we understood Him*, praying only for knowledge of His will for us and the power to carry that out.
12. Having had a spiritual awakening as the result of these steps, we tried to carry this message to alcoholics, and to practice these principles in all our affairs.

Twelve Steps from the book *Alcoholics Anonymous*, © 1939, 1955, 1976, Alcoholics Anonymous World Services, Inc. Reprinted by permission.

THE TWELVE STEPS OF
SEX AND LOVE ADDICTS
ANONYMOUS

1. We admitted we were powerless over sex and love addiction—that our lives had become unmanageable.
2. Came to believe that a Power greater than ourselves could restore us to sanity.
3. Made a decision to turn our will and our lives over to the care of God as we understood God.
4. Made a searching and fearless moral inventory of ourselves.
5. Admitted to God, to ourselves, and to another human being the exact nature of our wrongs.
6. Were entirely ready to have God remove all these defects of character.
7. Humbly asked God to remove our shortcomings.
8. Made a list of all persons we had harmed, and became willing to make amends to them all.
9. Made direct amends to such people wherever possible, except when to do so would injure them or others.
10. Continued to take personal inventory and when we were wrong promptly admitted it.
11. Sought through prayer and meditation to improve our conscious contact with God as we understood God, praying only for knowledge of God's will for us and the power to carry that out.
12. Having had a spiritual awakening as a result of these steps, we tried to carry this message to sex and love addicts, and to practice these principles in all areas of our lives.

Reprinted with permission of the Augustine Fellowship, *Sex and Love Addicts Anonymous* (Boston: The Augustine Fellowship Press, 1986).

I will now share some of my experience with the steps.

Step One

As a feminist, I had a terrible time with Step One. I came to a screeching halt at the word "powerless." Hence, I was stuck at "pre–Step One" for some time. I had dealt with the powerlessness of women in this society and in the world, and never again was I going to be powerless. After some years (I was *quite* stubborn!), I came to see that Step One was not about personal powerlessness, it was about control or, more accurately speaking, my illusion of control. Also, it does not say that I am powerless as a person. It says that I am powerless *over my addiction.* That is the definition of addiction. An addiction is something that has us. I came to see that being powerless over my addiction was much different from being powerless as a person. In fact, admitting that I was powerless over my addiction increased my personal power and offered me a tremendous relief from my illusion of control. Seeing my life as having become unmanageable was easy. One can only deny reality for so long. Then came Step Two.

Step Two

First I had to admit that I was *insane.* That took some doing. I really could control my life . . . back to Step One.

Any addiction is insanity. As Carnes says: "An essential part of sanity is being grounded in reality, so in the sense that addicts distort reality, the sexual addiction becomes a form of insanity."[8] Me insane? Hardly. Slowly, I came to see that what I had thought was love was a form of insanity. "Real" lovers are willing to destroy their lives for the sake of their love. (Now, really!) Elvira Madigan did not do much with hers.[9] I was not willing to go that route.

So I could admit that I was insane *when I was in my disease.* Everyone else could see it. It's so funny the way we think we can hide our disease. It is obvious, especially to those who are recovering. Perhaps this is why people who are not recovering do not like to be around those who are. Who knows?

Then I heard someone say that Step Two can be seen thus: "I came"—I had to arrive at a place where I wanted to recover. "I came to"—recovery is "coming to," seeing our disease and seeing what it is doing to our lives. "I came to believe"—I do believe, and I spent years in seminary intellectualizing what I believed in. "A power greater than myself"—I did not have much trouble with that; I knew there were powers greater than myself. "Could restore me to sanity"—sure. Why not? Whew. Step Two was done for the time being.

Step Three

This step was another test of my willingness to give over my illusion of control. I had seen the term *God* so distorted and used for violence that I became stuck on that for some time. It gave me a great opportunity to look at my stubbornness. Finally, I settled for the term *The Process of the Universe*. Step Three is a constant challenge.

Step Four

Whew! This one took work. It had to be written down. I had to look carefully at all the things I had done and see the role of my disease in them. Thank God, I was no older than I was when I did this step! By this time, I had seen the changes that had taken place in me as I did the other steps, so I was able to take this one seriously and do it carefully.

Step Five

I have always been a person who is "out there" with myself. Yet I discovered that even I had some unshared feelings, thoughts, and behaviors. This is a step I repeat (like the others) every day of my life. In the Twelve-Step Program, they say, "We are as sick as the secrets we keep." I believe it.

Step Six

This one looked easy. My brain said, "Of course," and my addiction said, "Now, wait a minute. Do you really want to give up

your illusion of control, your stubbornness, your dualisms?"
Back to Step One. Then I saw that the step said "*ready* to have
God remove my defects." I did not have to give them up yet. I
could work on *getting ready*. Needless to say, this took some time.
Meanwhile, I found that my life was working better.

During this entire time, it was always easy for me to jump to
Step Twelve—I know how to help others!

Step Seven

Now I have to leap off the cliff. No more getting ready. Oh,
well, why not?

Step Eight

This one was not so difficult for me. I grew up in a family that
lived this way and found that I was up-to-date on much of my
making of amends. As I focused on this step, however, I uncovered some hidden ones.

Step Nine

Mostly this step was a relief. Sometimes I got into trouble in
trying to "force" my amends.

Also, I had to realize that I was making amends for myself and
for my recovery. I was *not* seeking forgiveness. That was irrelevant to my recovery. When I focused on trying to get forgiveness,
it was back to Step One.

Step Ten

This is a great step for me. I really love it. It is like a fresh spring
breeze or wading into sparkling water. If we have done our work
to this point, this step almost does itself. At least, it has been that
way for me. I realized the self-centeredness of guilt and shame
and just do not like to feel them. Some people get upset when I
do not feel shame and guilt when I have made a "mistake." This
is not my problem. I do not have the energy to indulge. I have
too much living to do.

Step Eleven

By this time, I did not jump on the hooks of the language. I know to live my process. I need alone time and time for "prayer and meditation." I seek these times and welcome these times, knowing that they sustain me.

Step Twelve

Of course, this is not evangelism. This step is giving information and being present as a clear, sober person in touch with my whole being. I can do that. It feels good, and others even seem to benefit from this process. Whoopee!

After much critical consternation, I tried the steps and they worked. It is so simple. It is like putting on new glasses; those who wear these glasses can see the world from a different perspective.

More About Recovery

There are only a few more things I want to say with respect to recovery. During early recovery from this constellation of addictions, it is necessary to maintain abstinence from the addictive agent and behavior. To pseudo-relationship addicts this often sounds as though they will never to able to have any relationship of any kind for the rest of their lives! Abstinence does not mean that. It means that one is not ready to attempt any genuinely intimate relationships during early recovery, which is usually two to five years.

For the sexual addict, this means complete abstinence from their addictive sexual behavior, which usually translates into *no sexual behavior*.

For the romance addict, this may mean no movies or other triggers for the romance addiction. It also means no involvement in "romantic" relationships.

For the relationship addict, this usually means withdrawing from all relationships that are *a* relationship; that is, any place the illusion is trying to make *a* relationship.

For all three, it means abstaining from what have been called intimate, coupled, committed relationships. Addicts in this constellation (and most others too, probably) have no skills at *real* intimate relationships, but this does not mean that they have not been trying. It's time to quit trying for a while and focus upon one's own personal recovery. Is it too much to ask? Some people think so, but I know of no other way.

This is a time to let go of the frantic pressure to get the fix and establish relationships. This is a time for healing, a time for coming together inside. This does not mean that existing relationships have to be terminated. The focus on them must be laid aside until some sobriety has been established. Then it will be time enough to see if there *is* a relationship, if it was only two addictions meeting, or if the individuals want to begin something new. This can all happen later.

This need not to focus on relationship does not mean, however, that the recovering person should or needs to be isolated. Far from it. Never has the need for support and friendship been greater. The Twelve-Step Program meets this need. (I refer you to *Sex and Love Addicts Anonymous*; read the entire book again and again.) Also, it is important to have one or more sponsors during early recovery. They can be there for you.

Most addicts who have focused upon relationship skills for their addictions do not have many friends and really do not know how to make or to be a friend. This is a time for friendship. This is a time for learning friendship skills. This is a time to learn that intimate relationships are built upon friendship and that friendship skills are different than those learned in these addictions.

During this time the need for clear touching and physical contact may be important. It will be up to each person to know what threatens her or his sobriety; hugs, squeezes, even therapeutic nonsexual massage may be very important. Recovering persons should take good care of themselves.

Along with the healing from the addictions(s), this can be an important time for other physical healing such as improving one's diet, exercise, and skin care, and indulging in extravagances like soaking in a tub or a hot spring. Take care, and take good care of yourself during early recovery.

As the sedating effect of the addictions is removed, many feelings and memories that have been held down by the addiction will emerge. It is important to pay attention to these and find safe places to work them through. We can share these feelings in twelve-step groups, and these groups are not really designed to work them through.

With all the addictions described in this book it is not unusual for incest memories to emerge, since there seems to be a linkage between the pseudo-relationship addictions and incest. It takes careful, nonintrusive facilitation to be with someone through these times. I believe the Living Process Facilitation that I have been teaching throughout the world works best, and I am sure that there are other approaches that prove helpful. Most important is that the person being with you through this process is relatively clear, does not control and manipulate you, stays out of the way, and does not have his or her own ax to grind in the form of unresolved issues. The wrong kind of person or approach not only will not help, it will probably impede your recovery process.

A Final Word

Many years ago a famous Jewish theologian, Martin Buber, wrote a book about relationships called *I and Thou*.[10] He described the usual kind of relationship that we have as an I–It relationship, in which we treat the other like an inanimate object to be controlled and manipulated to "meet our needs." He was, I believe, talking about addictive relationships and how they operate. (Although they could more accurately be described as It–It relationships in his terminology.)

The I–Thou is a covenant relationship, which is exemplified by the kind of relationship one imagines having with one's God process. In that kind of relationship, both or all persons involved have a relationship that is expanding, in process, done with respect, a process that facilitates spirituality and is alive and living. No one is treated like an object, neither the self nor the other. In fact, there is a recognition and an experience of oneness.

The self and others are treated as Thous to be honored and respected. I believe that his I–Thou concept is another way of describing sobriety. When we are operating out of our sobriety (spirituality-process) all life, including our own, is treated like a Thou, and relationships are reflective of the sacred. We all have this possibility if we are willing to face our addictions and recover. Paradoxically, our escape from intimacy may have led us into Thouness with ourselves and all the universe. If we do our recovery process, it is so simple. It is not always easy.

Notes

Introduction

1. Patrick Carnes, *Out of the Shadows: Understanding Sexual Addiction* (Minneapolis: CompCare, 1985), p. 19.
2. *Sex and Love Addicts Anonymous* (Boston: The Augustine Fellowship Press, 1986).
3. Anne Wilson Schaef, *Co-Dependence: Misunderstood, Mistreated* (San Francisco: Harper & Row, 1986).
4. Carnes, p. 56.

Chapter One: Sexual Addiction

1. Carnes, *Out of the Shadows*, p. 4.
2. Charlotte Eliza Kasl, Ph.D., *Women and Sexual Addiction* (Minneapolis, MN: 1984), pp. 5, 7, 8.
3. Carnes, pp. 28, 37.
4. Ibid, p. 37.
5. Ibid., p. 45.
6. Ibid., pp. 26–51.
7. Ibid., p. 80.
8. Kasl, *Women and Sexual Addiction*, p. 1.
9. Carnes, p. 64.
10. Kasl, p. 1.
11. Sharon Wegscheider-Cruse, *Another Chance: Hope & Health for the Alcoholic Family* (Palo Alto, CA: Science & Behavior Books, 1980). The roles of Hero Child, Scapegoat, Lost Child, and Mascot.
12. Donald E. MacNamara and Edward Sagarin, *Sex, Crime, and the Law* (New York: The Free Press, 1978).
13. Carnes, p. 72.

Chapter Three: Relationship Addiction

1. Carnes, *Out of the Shadows*, p. 9.
2. Philip D. Eastman, *Are You My Mother?* (New York: Random House, 1960).
3. Sandra Felt, M.S.W., a former trainee, friend, and excellent living process facilitator.

Chapter Four: Escape from Intimacy

1. Carnes, *Out of the Shadows*, p. ii.
2. Earnie Larsen, Tape on co-dependence. Available from Earnie Larsen, Minneapolis.

3. *Sex and Love Addicts Anonymous* (Boston: Augustine Fellowship Press, 1986), pp. 74, 75.

4. Anne Wilson Schaef, *When Society Becomes an Addict* (San Francisco: Harper & Row, 1987).

Chapter Five: Addictive Relationships

1. Stanton Peele, *Love and Addiction* (New York: Taplinger, 1975); Colette Dowling, *The Cinderella Complex* (New York: Pocket Books, 1981); Dan Kiley, *The Peter Pan Syndrome* (New York: Dodd, Mead, 1983); Robin Norwood, *Women Who Love Too Much* (New York: Pocket Books, 1985); Susan Forward and Joan Torres, *Men Who Hate Women and the Women Who Love Them* (New York: Bantam, 1985).

2. Anne Wilson Schaef, *Women's Reality* (San Francisco: Harper & Row, 1986), p. 58.

Chapter Six: Intimacy and Healthy Relationships

1. Jed Diamond, *Looking for Love in All the Wrong Places* (New York: Putnam, 1988).

2. Schaef, *Women's Reality*.

3. Diane Fassel, Ph.D., friend and co-author of *The Addictive Organization* (San Francisco: Harper & Row, 1988).

Chapter Seven: Recovery

1. Carnes, *Out of the Shadows*, p. 56.

2. *Sex and Love Addicts Anonymous*, p. 119.

3. Kasl, *Women and Sexual Addiction*, p. 37.

4. Carnes, p. 10.

5. Melody Beattie, *Co-dependent No More* (New York: Harper/Hazelden, 1987), pp. 169, 170.

6. Augustine Fellowship Staff, *Sex and Love Addicts Anonymous*, (Boston, MA: Augustine Fellow, 1986).

7. *Alcoholics Anonymous*, "The Big Book," 3d ed. (New York: Alcoholics Anonymous World Services, 1976).

8. Carnes, p. 5.

9. *Elvira Madigan*, Screenplay by Bo Widerberg, Directed by Bo Widerberg, Atlantic Releasing Corp., 1981. Thorm/Emi Video.

10. Martin Buber, *I and Thou* (New York: Scribner, 1958).

Bibliography

Alcoholics Anonymous, "The Big Book." 3d ed. New York: Alcoholics Anonymous World Services, 1976.

Bach, Richard. *Bridge Across Forever*. New York: Morrow, 1984.

Backus, William, and Marie Chapian. *Telling Yourself the Truth*. Minneapolis: Bethany Fellowship, 1980.

Baer, Jean. *How to Be an Assertive (Not Aggressive) Woman in Life, in Love, and on the Job*. New York: New American Library, 1976.

Barry, Kathleen. *Female Sexual Slavery*. New York: New York Univ. Press, 1984.

Beattie, Melody. *Co-Dependent No More*. New York: Hazelden, 1987.

Becker, Ernest. *The Denial of Death*. New York: The Free Press, 1973.

Bellah, Robert, Richard Madsen, William Sullivan, Ann Swidler, and Steven Tipton. *Habits of the Heart: Individualism and Commitment in American Life*. Berkeley: Univ. of California Press, 1985.

Bernikow, Louise. *Alone in America: The Search for Companionship*. New York: Harper & Row, 1986.

Black, Claudia. *It Will Never Happen to Me!* New York: Macmillan, 1972.

Bloomfield, Harold. *Making Peace With Your Parents*. New York: Random House, 1983.

Blos, Peter. *The Adolescent Passage*. New York: International Universities Press, 1979.

Branden, Nathaniel. *Honoring the Self: Personal Integrity and the Heroic Potentials of Human Nature*. Boston: Houghton Mifflin, 1983.

Buber, Martin. *I and Thou*. New York: Scribner, 1958.

Bugental, J. F. T. *The Search for Existential Identity*. San Francisco: Jossey-Bass, 1976.

Carnes, Patrick. *Contrary to Love, Understanding Sexual Addiction, Part 2: Helping the Sexual Addict*. Minneapolis: CompCare Publications, in press.

———. *Out of the Shadows: Understanding Sexual Addiction*. Minneapolis: CompCare, 1985.

———. *The Sexual Addiction*. Minneapolis: CompCare, 1983.

Crawford, Linda, and Lee Lanning. *Loving: Women Talk About Their Love Relationships*. Minneapolis: Midwest Health Center for Women, 1981.

Crum, Tom. *The Magic of Conflict*. New York: Simon & Schuster, 1987.

Diamond, Jed. *Looking for Love in All the Wrong Places*. New York: Putnam, 1988.

Dinnerstein, Dorothy. *The Mermaid and the Minotaur: Sexual Arrangements and Human Malaise*. New York: Harper & Row, 1976.

Dowling, Colette. *The Cinderella Complex: Women's Hidden Fear of Independence*. New York: Pocket Books, 1981.

Driggs, John H. "Relationships." Minneapolis: *The Phoenix*, July 1984.

Dyer, Wayne W. *Your Erroneous Zones*. New York: Funk & Wagnalls, 1976.

Eastman, Philip D. *Are You My Mother?* New York: Random House, 1960.

Ehrenreich, Barbara. *The Hearts of Men: American Dreams and the Flight from Commitment*. New York: Anchor Press/Doubleday, 1983.

Eichenbaum, Luise, and Susie Orbach. *What Do Women Want? Exploding the Myth of Female Dependency*. New York: Coward, McCann & Geoghegan, 1983.

Eisler, Riane. *The Chalice and the Blade*. New York: Harper & Row, 1987.

Ferguson, Charles. *The Male Attitude*. Boston: Little, Brown, 1966.

Forward, Susan, and Joan Torres. *Men Who Hate Women and the Women Who Love Them*. New York: Bantam, 1985.

Goldberg, Herb. *The Hazards of Being Male: Surviving the Myth of Masculine Privilege*. New York: New American Library, 1976.

———. *The Inner Male: Overcoming Roadblocks to Intimacy*. New York: New American Library, 1987.

———. *The New Male-Female Relationship*. New York: Morrow, 1983.

Gordon, Barbara. *Jennifer Fever: Older Men—Younger Women*. New York: Harper & Row, 1988.

Grosz, George. *Love Above All*. New York: Shocken Books, 1985.

Halpern, Howard M. *How to Break Your Addiction to a Person*. New York: Bantam Books, 1982.

Hite, Shere. *Women and Love, A Cultural Revolution in Progress*. New York: Alfred A. Knopf, 1987.

Hodgson, Ray. *Self-watching: Addictions, Habits, Compulsions, What to Do About Them*. New York: Facts on File, 1982.

Hollis, Judi. *Fat Is a Family Affair*. San Francisco: Harper/Hazelden, 1986.

———. *Hope and Recovery: A Twelve-Step Guide for Healing from Compulsive Sexual Behavior*. Minneapolis: CompCare, 1987.

Jampolsky, Gerald. *Love Is Letting Go of Fear*. Berkeley, CA: Celestial Arts, 1979.

———. *Teach Only Love*. New York: Bantam, 1983.

Kasl, Charlotte Eliza. *Women and Sex Addiction*, Minneapolis: 1984.

Kaufman, Barry Neil. *To Love Is to Be Happy With*. New York: Fawcett Crest, 1978.

Keller, Catherine. *From a Broken Web: Separation, Sexism and Self.* Boston: Beacon Press, 1986.

Kiley, Dan. *The Peter Pan Syndrome: Men Who Have Never Grown Up.* New York: Dodd, Mead, 1983.

———. *The Wendy Dilemma: When Women Stop Mothering Their Men.* New York: Arbor House, 1984.

Kimball, Bonnie-Jean. *The Alcoholic Woman's Mad, Mad World of Denial and Mind Games.* Center City, MN: Hazelden Educational Materials, 1978.

Larsen, Earnie. *Stage II Relationships: Love Beyond Addiction.* San Francisco: Perennial Library, 1987.

Lasch, Christopher. *The Culture of Narcissism: American Life in an Age of Diminishing Expectations.* New York: Norton, 1978.

Levertov, Denise. "Divorcing." In *Freeing of the Dust.* New York: New Directions, 1975.

Lewis, Helen Block. *Psychic War in Men and Women.* New York: New York Univ. Press, 1976.

Lifton, Robert Jay. *Boundaries: Psychological Man in Revolution.* New York: Random House, 1969.

MacNamara, Donald E., and Edward Sagarin. *Sex, Crime and the Law.* New York: The Free Press, 1978.

Maslow, Abraham H., ed. *Motivation and Personality*, 2d ed. New York: Harper & Row, 1970.

May, Rollo. *Power and Innocence: A Search for the Sources of Innocence.* New York: Norton, 1972.

McCabe, Thomas R. *Victims No More.* Center City, MN: Hazelden Educational Materials, 1978.

Miller, Alice. *For Your Own Good.* New York: Farrar, Straus, Giroux, 1984.

Miller, William R. *The Addictive Behaviors.* New York: Pergamon Press, 1980.

Norwood, Robin. *Letters from Women Who Love Too Much.* New York: Pocket Books, 1985.

———. *Women Who Love Too Much.* New York: Pocket Books, 1985.

Paul, Jordon, and Margaret Paul. *Do I Have to Give Up Me to Be Loved By You?* Minneapolis: CompCare, 1984.

———. *Free to Love.* Los Angeles: Evolving Publications, 1983.

———. *From Conflict to Caring.* Minneapolis: CompCare, 1988.

———. *If You Really Loved Me.* Minneapolis: CompCare, 1987.

Peele, Stanton. *Love and Addiction.* New York: Taplinger, 1975.

Person, Ethel Spector. *Dreams of Love and Fateful Encounters: The Power of Romantic Passion.* New York: Norton, 1988.

Powell, John S. *Why Am I Afraid to Tell You Who I Am?* Allen, TX: Argus Communications, 1969.

Ray, Sondra. *I Deserve Love*. Millbrae, CA: Leo Femmes Publishing, 1976.

Restak, Richard M. *The Self Seekers*. Garden City, NY: Doubleday, 1982.

Rhodes, Sonya. *Cold Feet: Why Men Don't Commit*. New York: Dutton, 1988.

Rosellini, Gayle, and Mark Worden. *Of Course You're Angry*. San Francisco: Harper/Hazelden, 1986.

Robin, Lillian. *Intimate Strangers: Men and Women Together*. New York: Harper & Row, 1983.

Rubin, Theodore I. *Reconciliations: Inner Peace in an Age of Anxiety*. New York: The Viking Press, 1980.

Rue, James J., and Louise Shanahan. *Daddy's Girl, Mama's Boy*. New York: New American Library, 1978.

Russianoff, Penelope. *Why Do I Think I Am Nothing Without a Man?* New York: Bantam, 1982.

Schaef, Anne Wilson. *Co-Dependence: Misunderstood, Mistreated*. San Francisco: Harper & Row, 1986.

———. *When Society Becomes an Addict*. San Francisco: Harper & Row, 1987.

———. *Women's Reality: An Emerging Female System in a White Male Society*. San Francisco: Harper & Row, 1986.

———, and Diane Fassel. *The Addictive Organization*. San Francisco: Harper & Row, 1988.

Schaeffer, Brenda. *Is It Love or Is It Addiction: Falling Into Healthy Love*. New York: Harper & Row, 1987.

Sex and Love Addicts Anonymous. Boston: The Augustine Fellowship Press, 1986.

Shaevitz, Morton. *Sexual Static: How Men Are Confusing the Women They Love*. Boston: Little, Brown, 1987.

Shain, Merle. *Hearts That We Broke Long Ago*. New York: Bantam Books, 1983.

Sheehy, Gail. *Passages: Predictable Crises in Adult Life*. New York: Dutton, 1974.

Siegel, Bernie. *Love, Medicine and Miracles*. New York: Harper & Row, 1986.

Steiner, Claude M. *What Do You Say After You Say Hello?* New York: Grove Press, 1972.

Tennov, Dorothy. *Love and Limerance*. New York: Stein & Day, 1978.

Tschirhart-Sanford, Linda, and Mary Ellen Donovan. *Women and Self-Esteem*. New York: Viking Penguin, 1984.

Wegscheider-Cruse, Sharon. *Another Chance: Hope and Health for the Alcoholic Family*. Palo Alto, CA: Science & Behavior Books, 1980.

———. *Choicemaking: For Co-Dependents, Adult Children and Spirituality Seekers*. Pompano Beach, FL: Health Communications, 1985.

Wholey, Dennis. *The Courage to Change*. Boston: Houghton Mifflin, 1984.

Woititz, Janet Geringer. *Struggle for Intimacy*. Pompano Beach, FL: Health Communications, 1985.

York, Phyllis, David Wachtel, and Ted Wachtel. *Toughlove*. Garden City, NY: Doubleday, 1982.